BEERS

OF THE
WORLD

BILL YENNE

BEERS
OF THE
WORLD

BILL YENNE

CHARTWELL
BOOKS, INC.

4

Published by
BOOK SALES, INC.
114 Northfield Avenue
Raritan Center
Edison, N.J. 08818

Produced by
Brompton Books Corp.
15 Sherwood Place
Greenwich, CT 06830

ISBN 0-7858-0020-4

Printed in China

Designed by Tom Debolski

Reprinted 1995

Designed by Tom Debolski

PAGE ONE: An example of nineteenth-century Bohemian and Bavarian glass and pewter steins from the collection of the Staropramen Brewery in Prague.

PREVIOUS PAGES: A classic view of golden lager and golden grain. A component of the Fischer Group, Brasserie du Pêcheur brews the group's flagship beer at Schiltigheim in the Alsace region of France.

ACKNOWLEDGEMENTS:

The author would like to gratefully acknowledge all of the breweries' generosity in providing the labels and information for this book. The author would also like to thank Ruth DeJauregui and Lynne Piade for their help in researching this book. In addition, the following individuals provided invaluable assistance: Roger Stuhlmuller at Acme Food Specialties; Don Shook of Adolph Coors; Dr Júrgen Auckenthaler at Adambräu Gesellschaft; Paul I Nunny at Adnams and Company; Michael Buckner of Albuquerque Brewing; Alken-Maes Brouwerijen Brasseries; Gill Freshwater at Allied Breweries; Carl Glauner at Alpirsbacher Klosterbräu; Gibbs Mewple at Anchor Brewery; Mark Carpenter and Fritz Maytag of Anchor Brewing; Carl Bolz and George Westin of Anheuser-Busch; Toshisuke Zako at Asahi; Sarah Koh and Judy Long at Asia Pacific Breweries; HB Kalavar at Associated Breweries & Distilleries; AF Huberts of Banjul Breweries; Jodi A Pilotto at Barton Beers; Lesley Wardle of Bass Breweries; Robert Peyton of Basso & Associates; Wiebke Kobbe of Bavaria-St Pauli-Bräuerei; Michael Tassin at Belukus Marketing; Mr Beyer at Berliner Kindle Bräuerei; M Weber at Bières de Chimay; M Breuer and M Wrobel at Binding-Bräuerei; V Moro at Birra Moretti; Michael Meinardus at Bitburger Pils; Paul Summers of Blue Ridge Brewing; Frie van de Wouw of Bofferding; Jim Koch of Boston Beer Company.

Jean-Pierre Eloir at Brasserie de l'Abbaye Des Rocs; Chris Bauweraerts at Brasserie D'Achouffe; Ms MN Pourtois at Brasserie de Blaugies; Marie André Cherty at Brasserie Dubuisson Frères; Oliver Debus, Valentine Brau and Roger Knauss at Brasserie Fischer; Dominique Friart at Brasserie Friart; Simon Berdugo of Brasserie Jeanne d'Arc; François Entz at Brasserie Meteor; Charles Fontaine at Brasserie de Silly; Gunter Graefenhain at Brau & Brunnen USA; Kristine Deicke at Bräuerei Aying; Dr HW Dietel of Bräuerei Cluss; Caroline Schaller at Bräuerei zum Gurten; Marie Peacock of Brick Brewing; Robin Hinz of BridgePort Brewing; Stephen Hindy of the Brooklyn Brewery; Antoine Bosteels at Brouwerij Bosteels Brasserie; R Anthonissen at Brouwerij Haacht; Miel Mattheus at Brouwerij De Kluis; Annemie Craenen, Hilde Juressen and Fons Martens at Brouwerij Martens; Claudia De Maeyer at Brouwerij Moortgat; L Piessens at Brouwerij Piessens; Etienne Detailleur at Brouwerij Riva; Peter Doclo and J Snauwaert at Brouwerij Roman; Jan Coupe at Brouwerij De Smedt; Maree Bylett at The Cascade Brewery Co; Antoine Boyer Chammard at Brasserie Nouvelle de Lutèce; Pat Samson and Catherine Van Evans of Carling O'Keefe; Ole Andreasen at Carlsberg A/S; Suzanne Howell at Carlsberg Brewery; Harley Madsen at Carlsberg International; Karen McKeering of Castlemaine Perkins Limited; Alan Davis of Catamount Brewing; Marco AH-Mar of Cervecería Cuauhtemoc; Jose Paz Aguirre of Cervecería Moctezuma; Roman De Wenter of Cold Spring Brewing; Mike Lanzarotta of the Crown City Brewery.

James Degnan of Degnan Associates; U Brodbbeck and G Guder at Dinkelacker Bräuerei; Jeff Ware of Dock Street; Kris Herteleer at De Dolle Brouwers; Helene Klein at Dortmunder Actien-Bräuerei; Cindy Wynn at Dribeck Importers; Michael Jaeger of Dubuque Star; Evelyn Wood at EFCO Importers; Barbaros Şaylan of Efes Pilsen Group; Holger Klapproth of Einbecker Brauhaus; Enrique Solaeres Rodríguez at El Aguila; Mr Rauschert at Erste Kulmbacher Actienbräuerei; Irmtraut Hirschfeld and Felicitas Schlué of Feldschlösschen; Jacques Le Grip at Fischer Beverages International; Jeff Davis of Fleishman Hillard; Ferdinand M Schumacher at Frankenmuth Brewery; Thomas Jones of Genesee Brewing; M Sweet at Gibbs Mew; S Nemeth and H Zentgraf at Gilde Bräuerei; Gerald Feck at Gösser worldwide; Janet ter Ellen at Grolsch Export; Judith Austin and Leonie Brennan at Guinness; Paul Rutten at Gulpener Bierbrouwerij; Brian Miller at Hall

& Woodhouse; Nadeen Gonzalez at Hans Holterbosch; Kari Wulf at Hansa Bryggeri; Peter Cook at Heaven Hill Distilleries; Annemiek Louwers at Heineken Internationaal Beheer; HV Seidel and St Fischlein at Heylands Bräuerei; Klaus-Henning Ost at Hofbräu München; P O'Connor and A Lakebrink of Holsten-Bräuerei; Wenzel Hintermeier of Hüchelner Brauhaus; R Gyger and P Knobel at Hürlimann; Gerard Fauchey, A Hanin and Jud Kerkhof at Interbrew; Andreas Didion, Robert Hess and Ingrid Zabransky of Karlsberg Bräuerei; Mrs Muthoni Muthiga of Kenya Breweries; Michelle Grubman at Kirin USA; Günter Heyden of Krombacher Bräuerei; Kathleen Fogarty, Karen Patching and Samantha Ward of Labatt; Suzanne Lanza; J Louwaege at Louwaege Gebroeders; Brewwood International for Maccabee; Philip Merrit of Manhattan Brewing; Didier Vallet at Mauritius Breweries; Charles Finkel and Maria Hall at Merchant Du Vin; Steven Forsyth and Jeff Waalkes of Miller Brewing; Charles Cooney, Jr, Curator, Milwaukee County Historical Society; KK Mittu at Mohan Meakin; Hugh Coppen, Harley Deeks and Barbara M Paterno at Molson Breweries USA; Deanna Gallaway, Rhonda Rogers and at Moosehead; Marc Bishop at Morland & Company.

Tom Allen of North Coast Brewing; Dr Herman Regusters at Ngok' Imports; JC Nwoboshi of Nigerian Breweries; Owen O'Connor at O'Connor O'Sullivan Advertising; John F Phillips at Olde Time Brewers; Joe Shields of the Oldenberg Brewery; Tom Venho at Olvi Oy; J Rautek of Oranjeboom Bierbrouwerij; Ritva Kyynäräinen of Oy Sinebrychoff; Helmut Lindinger, A Seidl and R Gimpl at Österreichische Brau; Doris Haitzer at Ottakringer Bräuerei Harmer; Tapani Ilmanen at Oy Hartwall; Kaarina Linnanen at Oy Mallasjuoma; Barry Lazarus of Pacific Coast Brewing; George Saxon at Phoenix Imports; Jaroslav Soucek at Pilsner Urquell; Marita Niedenzu at Privatbräuerei Diebles; K Dürr at Privatbräuerei Gebr Gatzweiler; W van Rooij of Raaf; Thomas Wölfel of Reichelbräu; Mary Thompson of Reinheitsgebot; Amund Ringnes at Ringnes; Christa Lannoo-De Clippel at RIVA Group; Gail Rolka.

Merja Niomenen at Saate/Tiedotus; Alan Paul of San Francisco Brewing; Arturo R Cuevas at San Miguel; Maiko Ishida at Sapporo Breweries; Eleanor Nakagawa at Sapporo USA; Stacy Saxon of the Saxon Brewery; Greg Schirf of Schirf Brewing; A Prokoph at Schwaben Bräu; Ken at Scottish & Newcastle Importers; C Inglin and M Levrat at Sibra; Paul Camusi and Steve Harrison of Sierra Nevada; Silvia Fadda at Sociedad Anónima Dammi; Geraldine Scott at The South African Breweries; Denis O'Flynn at E Smithwick & Sons Ltd, St Francis Abbey Brewery; Kevin Taylor of The South Australian Brewing Company; Katrin Klein at Spaten-Franziskaner-Bräu; Andreas Hildebrandt at Spaten West; Chris Sherman of the St Petersburg Times; Brother Paul at St Sixtus Abdij; Jana Masínová at Staropramen; B Seidel of Staatliches Hofbräuhaus; Eric Vaughn Smith at Stawski Distributing; Peter Blum of Stroh Brewing; Masahide Kanzaki at Suntory; Melanie K Webster at The Swan Brewery; Ian Bradshaw at Tasmanian Breweries; Amos Meltzer of Tempo; Katie Bates of Tied House; J Van Antwerpen at Timmermans; Maree Middleton and Kate Windon of Tooheys; Jeffrey L Zeisler at The Traditional Beer Importing Company; Mr Aichele at Tucher Bräu; Ahmet Şükrü Yılmaz of Türk Tuborg; Sybil Brown at Upper Canada Brewing Company; Laura Rozza at Van Munching & Co; E Magnani at Vaux Breweries; Peggy Dudinyak of the Vernon Valley Bräuhaus; Vereinigte Kärntner Bräuereien at Villacher Bräuerei; Mr Beck of Warsteiner Bräuerei; J Hazelwood at The Whitbread Beer Company; Judy Wicks of the White Dog Cafe; Jim Ford of Widmer Brewing; Paul-Thomas Hinkel and Dieter Wagner of Würzburger Hofbräu; Bert Grant of Yakima Brewing; Joanne Lazusky of Yuengling; Ryszard Wróblewski at Zaklady Piwowarskie w Warszawie.

CONTENTS

INTRODUCTION

It is well known that beer was an essential part of life at the dawn of civilization and some scholars have gone so far as to picture it as one of the very cornerstones of that civilization. Indeed, Professor Solomon Katz of the University of Pennsylvania has advanced the theory that human kind first domesticated grain not to bake bread but to *brew beer*!

In 1989, Fritz Maytag and the Anchor Brewing Company in San Francisco created a stir in the American brewing community when they unveiled Ninkasi, a beer which was an attempt to 'duplicate humankind's earliest professionally brewed beer.' First presented at the Microbrewers Convention in September 1989 and available in the Bay Area for a few months thereafter, Ninkasi was a recreation of a Sumerian beer which had been brewed around 2800 BC. With the help of Professor Katz, Maytag introduced

The Hymn to Ninkasi, an ancient poem dating from 1800 BC and dedicated to the Sumerian goddess of brewing. The poem also included a recipe for Sumerian beer that dated back to perhaps 2800 BC. His curiosity piqued, Maytag decided to do what no modern brewer had ever done: devote the resources of a modern state-of-the-art brewery to actually brewing a beer based on a recipe that hadn't been used in centuries!

The result was an unhopped, honey-sweetened beer unlike anything we'd ever tasted. Moreover, Fritz Maytag's self-described 'essay' gave us a taste of a bygone era. For a moment, a room full of people well-versed in beers from other *places*, found themselves tasting beer from another *time*.

As Katz and Maytag suggested, brewing in the cradle of civilization can be dated to at least 2800 BC and perhaps earlier. They discovered that in those days the art of the

brewer and that of the baker were closely intertwined, and as Anchor's 1989 recreation showed, ancient beer was brewed with barley loaves (later known as *bappir*), which could be eaten as bread or thrown into the brew kettle as a sort of shortcut mash. The ancient Babylonian word for beer was *kas* (the root of Ninkasi), and it is seen in ancient tablets hardly more often than the word *kasninda*, meaning beer-loaf. The word for brewer was *lukasninda*, the 'man of the beer-loaf.' Most beers in those days were brewed primarily with barley, and archaeological excavations have revealed pottery containing remnants of barley and barley mash. Beers were also flavored (as was Anchor's Ninkasi) with both honey and syrups prepared from dates, figs or concentrates of fruit juices. It was the custom of the early Babylonians, as well as the Syrians, the Hittites, the Armenians and the Greeks to drink their beer from large jars using straws or tubes. This practice was, incidentally, borrowed by Maytag for the debut serving of his Ninkasi.

As is the case today, there were a variety of beer styles in the Babylon of nearly 5000 years ago. These included black beer (*kassi*), fine black beer (*kassag*), premium beer (*kassagasaan*) and a product that probably looked—if not tasted—a great deal like familiar beers such as Bass Ale or Maytag's own Anchor Liberty Ale. This was known as *kassig*, or red beer. There was also a beer flavored with spices known as *kasusasig* and a white beer called *kurungig*. Beer played an important part in the court life of the monarchs, and there was a special 'royal' beer called *kasnaglugal*. Beer was also offered in sacrifice to the gods, specifically Ningirsu.

LEFT: A toast before dinner in Assyria, sixth millennium BC. FACING PAGE: A toast before dinner in Munich, Germany, second millennium AD.

In the hierarchy of deities there was, of course, the goddess Ninkasi, who lived on Mount Sabu, a mythical place whose name meant the 'mountain of the tavern keeper.'

Brewing and baking were equally common activities in the households of ancient Egypt. Beer was just as much of a staple as the bread, and both were routinely made in the home.

The Egyptian word for brewer was *fty*, while the process of brewing itself was known as *th*. Beer itself was known as *hkt*, *hek*, or *hekt*. This word is probably an adaptation of the old Babylonian word *hiqu*, implying a mixture, notwithstanding the Egyptian belief—recorded in an inscription on the temple at Dendera—that identifies the goddess Hathor as the 'inventress of brewing.' At Hathor's side was the goddess Menqut—the 'goddess who makes beer'—who was pictured in a wall painting at Dendera in a pose reminiscent of the St Pauli Girl holding a pair of beer jars. The jackal-headed god Anubis was also pictured as being offered jars of beer.

The earliest Egyptian texts enumerate a variety of beer styles, including dark beer and iron beer (recalled with a tip of the hat to Pennsylvania's Iron City). Also mentioned were the intriguing 'garnished' beers known

ABOVE: The staff at the Reiningshaus brewery in Graz, Austria, in 1906. FACING PAGE, TOP: Dappled ponies deliver the lagers of Austria's Gösser. FACING PAGE: Munich's Löwenbräu Brewery as it appeared circa 1890.

as *hes* and *hktsty*, the beer of Nubia and perhaps a cousin to the Babylonia *kasusasig*.

Advertising slogans seem to have played an important role in describing the more commercial beers, for these were known by such appellations as 'friend's beer,' 'beer of the protector,' 'beer which does not sour' and 'beer of the goddess Maat.' Then there are two which we surely would like to have tasted: 'beer of eternity' and 'beer of truth.' Most beers were offered for sale publicly, often served in bowls by young women. Ancient Egyptian beer was almost exclusively brewed with barley, and some words for beer translate literally as barley wine.

One of the oldest Egyptian brewing recipes comes down to us in a translation by Zosimus of Panopolis, a chemist writing before the time of Photios:

'Take fine, clean barley and moisten it for one day and draw it off, or also lay it up in a windless place until morning, and again wet it for six hours. Cast it into a smaller perforated vessel and wet it and dry it until it shall become shredded, and when this is so, shake it in the sunlight until it falls apart... Next grind it and make it into loaves, adding leaven just like bread, and cook it rather raw, and whenever [the loaves] rise, dissolve sweetened water and strain through a strainer or light sieve... In baking the loaves, cast them into a vat with water and boil it a little in order that it may not froth nor become lukewarm, and draw up and strain it, and having prepared it, heat and examine it.'

Three kinds of barley—black, white and red—were used in this process, which recalls the bappir loaves used by the Sumerians and by Fritz Maytag in 1989. Apparently, when the bread was half-baked, it was broken into pieces, soaked for several days and placed into a fermentation vat large enough to hold a person, who would then stamp and mash it. The mixture was then strained through a basket and ultimately filtered into beer jars. It has also been suggested that Egyptian beer may have, on occasion, been flavored with honey, lavender, cedar or nutmeg, and that beer produced for, and often brewed by, 'ladies' was flavored with flowers.

As radical a notion as Dr Katz's theory may be, it is topped by Egyptologist and professional brewer James Death, who first wrote in 1886 that beer was 'one of the hitherto unknown leavens of Exodus.' In other words, over a century ago, Death became convinced that the Bible's Book of Exodus (Exod 12: 15-20) was talking about beer. He added that the admonition of Moses in Exodus chapter 12 to abstain from leavened bread during Passover was, in reality, also an admonition to abstain from beer. The fact that the consumption of wine is permitted indicates the higher level to which beer was relegated.

All of this of course implies that beer drinking was as frequently encountered among the Israelite slaves as it was among their Egyptian masters. According to Death, beer was simply another leavened product to be included in daily life along with 'light bread.' As we know, brewing was common in ancient Egypt, and it is not inconceivable that many Israelites were employed at breweries during their period of enslavement in Egypt and indeed that many Israelites maintained home breweries.

James Death was a brewer who also became something of a Middle East scholar while working as a consulting brewer and chemist at the Cairo Brewery in the Egyptian capital back when Egypt was enduring its tenure as a British protectorate. Having retired to 7 Oakley Crescent in London, Jim Death put pen to paper and began publishing articles in such trade publications as *The Brewers' Guardian*. In March 1887, he convinced the firm of Trubner & Company to publish his amazing story in book form.

Death begins by pointing out the similarities between leavened bread as it is described in the Bible and the beer loaves, or bappir, which were used throughout the ancient Middle East as a sort of 'just add water' shortcut substitute for mash in the brewing process. Death also reminds us that the Bible (Judg 6: 19-20) mentions boiling bread and pouring off a broth. He cited his own firsthand experience with Boosa, the native Egyptian beer, still common in the nineteenth century, which began with a baked cake of unleavened flour that was mixed with malt and water which turned overnight into a 'sloppy mess' with a high concentration of carbon dioxide and alcohol. One use of this 'beer' in early times was to leaven bread. Death goes on to suggest that the ancient Hebrew *machmetzeth* was actually the equivalent of Boosa.

Consumption of beer throughout history was considerable, and indeed records show that during Egypt's Middle Kingdom (about 1800 BC), 130 jars of beer were delivered *daily* to the royal court. At one point, it is recorded that the queen herself received five jars—the equivalent of at least that many full liter steins—in one day. Oh, to have been a fly on the wall during *that* splendid afternoon on the shores of the Nile!

In Archbishop Rolleston's scholarly study, *Concerning the Origin and Antiquity of Barley Wine*, published in 1750 and based on his review of texts from early times, he

LEFT: The essential ingredients, barley and hops, fresh with dew. FACING PAGE: A golden field of barley near Hamburg, Germany, and a temperature-controlled hop storage facility in Chico, California.

described ale or barley wine as being of far greater antiquity than was then generally supposed. 'It is very remarkable,' he wrote, 'that other creatures can labor and toil and still continue their cheerfulness without anything but what is just necessary to support their beings and keep them alive. This is not the case with men. They cannot hold out without some spirituous refreshment, some liquor to cheer them, that is stronger than simple water. I cannot think that Noah was the inventor of wine, but imagine he was taught to make it by the antediluvians who were eating and drinking and enjoying themselves when the flood came. The same need of refreshment which caused the invention of wine in that part of the world where man was first placed did very soon after in other countries produce other liquors which might have the same effect.'

Beer is undoubtedly a beverage of very great antiquity, and the Greek scholar Aeschylus (525-456 BC) confirms that it was known that the Egyptians had invented beer before wine was first made. People living in climates that were not conducive to growing grapes and who could not therefore produce wine, extracted liquors from other fruits or grains. Among all these variety there were none more common than those extracted from barley, which Xenophon (430-355 BC) and Aristotle (384-322 BC) (as quoted by Athenaeus) called barley wine. Archbishop Rolleston noted that the Greeks lived well and enjoyed a beverage that they called the 'liquor of life.' *Sabarum*, or *sabara*, was another name for barley wine among the Dalmatians and Pannonians. The word *sabarum* is certainly of Hebrew extraction, from which comes Sabazius, a name for Bacchus in some cultures, as mentioned by Aristophanes (257-180 BC). The Roman consul and scholar Pliny the Younger (62-113 AD) reckoned that at least 195 types of such beverages had been invented in Europe by the first century. That renown Latin scholar, St Jerome (340-420 AD), makes mention of ale, cider, mead and palm wine. *Cerevisia* was another Latin word used for barley wine. Pliny mentions this name and says that it was called this in Gaul. The Spanish and Portuguese words for beer—*cerveza* and *cerveja*—are certainly derived from *cerevisia*.

It is clear that in countries that were not fit for vineyards, such as Britain and Scandinavia, there was a strong and pleasant beverage made of barley. Athenaeus wrote in *Dio, the Academic* that it was invented for the benefit of the poor, who were not able to buy wine, but it did not continue as a beverage among the poor only. As improvements were made in malting and brewing, it was enjoyed by the rich as well. Other grains were also

ABOVE AND OPPOSITE: Adnams beers of Southwold amidst pleasant English seacoast and village pub settings. FACING PAGE, TOP AND RIGHT: The pubs of London. British pubs offer a congenial imbibing environment.

used, and Julian the Apostate referred to beer as 'the offspring of corn,' and called it 'wine without wine.'

A biography of St Columbanus (589-610 AD), noted that 'When the hour of refreshment approached, the minister of the refectory endeavored to serve the ale (*cervesiam*), which is bruised from the juice of wheat and barley, and which all the nations of the earth—except the Scordiscae and Dardans, who inhabit the borders of the ocean—Gaul, Britain, Ireland and Germany and others who are not unlike them in manners use.'

In Europe during the Middle Ages, each town had numerous breweries and a great deal of beer was consumed. Reliable estimates calculate that each inhabitant consumed up to 800 pints (300-400 liters) of beer per year. Beer was a major element in the medieval diet. The beer, which was boiled during the brewing process, was basically germ-free, which meant that it was a good alternative for the heavily polluted drinking water. This period of prosperity for the brewing industry reached its peak sometime around 1500, and beer was always sold in the immediate vicinity of the brewery.

Beer consumption decreased after 1650 because of the increasing price as a result of increased taxes, the decline in the quality of the product and the increasing popularity of other new products such as gin, wine, tea, coffee, milk and cocoa. The upper classes usually drank wine and the number of beer breweries decreased considerably after 1650.

The modern history of beer probably began with the development of pale ales in England at the end of the eighteenth century. They were not truly 'pale,' but rather were deep amber to reddish in color and are the true predecessors to the ales brewed today in Britain and western North America. They were called 'pale' because they were perhaps the first widely available non-opaque beers produced in Europe.

Perhaps the most important development in the history of brewing and beer styles occurred in about the 1830s in an area of central Europe that could be called the

ABOVE: Gerard Heineken got his start in 1864 when he took over the 272-year-old De Hooiberg Brewery. Today, Heineken's is the world's best known beer. LEFT: Holsten's brewery in Hamburg, Germany, circa 1910.

'Golden Triangle' because of the golden color of beer style invented there and because of the way this region's output had enriched the world's brewers. This triangle had its three corners roughly located at Munich, Germany; Vienna, Austria; and at Pilsen in the Czech Republic. It is worth noting that lager, now the world's best selling international beer style, originated in a triangle whose corners are discussed in three separate chapters of this book!

Prior to the dawn of the nineteenth century, beer was produced at low room temperature using top-fermenting yeast (*Saccharomyces cerevisiae*) or yeast that rose to the top of the fermenting vessel. In the early nineteenth century, brewers in the Golden Triangle undertook the widespread use of what is now known as *Saccharomyces carlsbergensis*, a yeast that 'precipitated' or sank to the bottom of the fermentation vessel. Another important difference between *Saccharomyces carlsbergensis* and *Saccharomyces cerevisiae* was that the former fermented at much colder—near freezing—temperatures and for a longer period of time (four rather than two weeks). Because this process required the beer to be put away in an ice cave or an iced storehouse for a month or so, the resulting beer style is known as 'lager,' from the German verb 'to store.'

Lager beers originated in colder climates where ice was readily available but soon spread in popularity throughout the world. Bottom-fermented *lager* contrasts with top-fermented *ale* in that it is generally (but not always) lighter in color and more transpar-

ent and that it is almost always served chilled. Each of the corners of the Golden Triangle has given its name to a particular style of lager. The most popular of the styles in the world is the Pilsen style, or pilsener. Also the lightest in color of the lager family, this style has been adopted by all the large, mass-market beers in North America, Australia and Asia, as well as by Heineken lager, the most widely recognized single brand in the world today.

The lager revolution that began in the Golden Triangle in the early nineteenth century spread quickly, especially after the advent of practical, artificial ice-making in the 1870s. By the end of the nineteenth cen-

BELOW: The brew kettle rendered as art by Hans Sommer. FACING PAGE: Bottled beer was common by 1880, and canned beer, first marketed in bottle-like cans, appeared in the 1930s.

tury, lager was far and away the leading beer style everywhere in the world except in Britain and Ireland, where ale and stout (both top-fermenting beers) were dominant.

The story of the brewing industry in Europe and North America during the first half of the twentieth century was marked by consolidation, as large breweries bought smaller breweries and became *larger* breweries. Thus, the overall number of breweries declined. The small, independent brewers in Europe also suffered mightily from two world wars. Meanwhile, in North America, a dozen years of Prohibition reduced the number of brewers to a small fraction of the total at the beginning of the century.

By the midpoint of the twentieth century, the Pilsen-style lager (pilsener) had emerged as the ubiquitous international beer style. Other, more complex and flavorful styles were rare and generally hard to find. In the

late 1970s, however, a renaissance in diversifying beer styles emerged among people who yearned for variety in the types of beer they enjoyed. This renaissance was characterized by the Campaign for Real Ale (CAMRA) in Britain and the microbrewery revolution in the United States, Canada and eventually the Netherlands, Australia and elsewhere.

In recent decades, the brewing industry in North America has introduced several product innovations in an effort to create a distinctive variation on their mass market lagers. Because the taste of North American mass market lagers is so subtle compared to other beer styles, the innovations had to be more implicit than explicit. In other words, any change that was made had to be something that didn't require taste to distinguish, but rather a barely perceptible difference that might be apparent by reading the label

or through the perception that the beer was 'less filling.' The first such innovation was low calorie, or 'light' beer, which was introduced in the 1970s. 'Dry' beer was a new product introduced in 1990. The former was very successful, while the latter, which was similar technically, failed to generate significant market share.

In 1993, the two largest brewing companies in Canada and the United States began to market 'ice' beer. Developed and patented by Labatt in Canada, ice beer is a pale lager which is quickly chilled to subfreezing temperatures after brewing but before final fermentation. The result is the formation of ice crystals in the beer, which are removed to produce a beer with roughly *twice* the alcohol content of typical mass market lagers.

The advent of microbreweries and brewpubs in the United States and certain parts of Canada during the 1980s was probably the most exciting event in the history of North American brewing since Prohibition was repealed in 1933. For the first time in over a century, the number of brewing companies in North America began to increase. In the United States the number of breweries stood at about 50 from the early 1960s until the early 1980s, but increased to 190 in 1988. It has more than doubled again since then. The microbrewery revolution has given North Americans a vastly wider selection of styles and varieties of fresh, domestically produced beers than has been available since the nineteenth century. It also signaled a return to the concept of regional, and even neighborhood, breweries, an idea that was thought to have perished at the end of World War II.

Unlike North America's regional breweries which attempted, and failed, to compete with the national brands in the 1950s and 1960s, today's smaller breweries brew specialty beers with unique characters and much richer flavors than any of the national brands. While these styles do not appeal to the same millions that buy the mass market brands, many have attracted large and enthusiastic followings.

Beer was an essential part of life at the dawn of civilization in the ancient Middle East. It tempered the lives and loves of the Sumerians, the Egyptians and perhaps even Moses himself. Humankind domesticated grain to bake bread and to brew beer. It is certain that beer played a role in defining the roots of civilized life and in all that has come to pass since.

CLOCKWISE FROM TOP RIGHT: Enjoying good friends, good times and good beer in Tokyo, Japan; at the San Francisco Brewing Company in California; at a party in Switzerland, and in a cozy Munich bierstube.

AFRICA
AND THE
MIDDLE EAST

Just as the cradle of civilization can be traced to northeastern Africa and the Middle East, so too do we look to these regions for the origin of beer and brewing. It has been discovered that the brewer's art was held in high esteem over 5000 years ago in both Egypt and Sumeria, and large quantities of beer in many beer styles were produced in both countries. As the centuries passed and European brewing traditions began to develop, beer styles evolved throughout sub-Saharan Africa that used maize and other indigenous plants. This led to the evolution of beer that was quite different than that

which evolved in Europe. Even in Egypt an indigenous style called *boosa* was developed among the bedouins.

In the nineteenth century, as colonialism encroached upon the peoples of what was then known as the 'dark continent,' mass-produced European beer was introduced. Imported beer was quickly augmented by the construction—by Europeans—of European-style breweries in Africa itself, notably in Nigeria, Kenya, South Africa and the Belgian Congo (now Zaire). With the power of the industrial revolution's technology behind them, the European brewers were

able to effect a major change in the tastes of the African people, and the traditional, native beers all but disappeared.

One of the first areas where European beer and brewing made inroads in Africa was in what is now South Africa. However, this brewing tradition, like that of North America during the same period, was for the pleasure of European settlers. In 1658, Jan van Riebeeck decided to start brewing in the Cape of Good Hope country near present-day Cape Town, but because yeast and hops had to be imported, his first beer was not very good. The first professional brewer arrived at the Cape in 1694, and a site for a brewery was approved on Simon van der Stel's farm in Newlands, because, as he said, it had 'the finest and best water available for this purpose.' Today there is a modern brewery at Newlands, still using water drawn from the same natural springs.

For more than two centuries brewing remained a cottage industry. In 1820, however, Jacob Letterstedt established Mariendahl Brewery at Newlands and after Germans landed in Natal in 1848, there was an increased demand for Cape beer. By 1860, the Mariendahl Brewery had 60 competitors, mainly Cloetes and Martienssens. Crowders Brewery and William Peel's Umlass Brewery opened in Durban after the British garrison arrived in Natal. In 1862, Anders Ohlsson arrived from Norway and bought the Mariendahl Brewery upon the death of Jacob Letterstedt. In 1883, Ohlsson built Anneberg

Beers of Africa: A hop farm in South Africa (LEFT), and a Mamba still-life from the Ivory Coast.

ABOVE: Friends getting together to enjoy a round or two of SAB's Castle Lager at a typical South African pub.

BELOW: SAB's well-equipped facility at Rosslyn is the largest brewing plant in the Southern Hemisphere.

Brewery. By 1889, Ohlsson had become the beer baron of South Africa and had either absorbed or eliminated much of his competition. Ohlsson's Cape Breweries, Ltd, producing Lion Beer, virtually controlled the brewing industry on the Cape. Meanwhile, aided by George Raw, Frederick Mead raised the necessary capital to buy William Peel's Umlass Brewery in Durban. With the gold rush in the Transvaal came a beer rush, and Charles Chandler set up the first Transvaal brewery, Union Breweries, in 1887 in Ophirton.

Chandler's most noteworthy competitor was the Castle Brewery, founded by Charles Glass, which was purchased in 1887 by Frederick Mead. This in turn led to the formation of South African United Breweries, Ltd. Mead knew that growth was essential, and a large, new building was erected in Johannesburg. The market growth from Mead's Johannesburg brewery was tremendous, and in 1895 he took on investors to form a new company, the South African Breweries, Ltd (SAB). In 1899, SAB entered the Cape market by purchasing the Martienssen Brewery in Cape Town. By this time, the Castle label had been adopted for all SAB beers, and soon this brand began to make inroads into Ohlsson's territory.

With his Lion brand having lost ground in the Cape, Ohlsson diverted his attention to the Witwatersrand and bought the Thomas Brewery. Until this time, the market had been in Johannesburg, Durban and Cape Town, but now SAB expanded to Port Elizabeth, Salisbury, Rhodesia (now Harare in what is now Zimbabwe), and to Bloomfontein in 1906. Because of its size, SAB and its Castle brand now had no real fear of opposition.

SAB made its first of many moves toward a merger with Ohlsson's Cape Breweries, but Anders Ohlsson rejected these overtures. Both SAB and Ohlsson went through a prosperous period, reaching an agreement which regulated their relations in the hotel and bar trade. Increased postwar taxation led to increased prices and to a measurable decrease in consumption. Finally, with the market down, Ohlsson's Cape Breweries and Union Breweries merged into SAB in 1956.

Today SAB is the leading brewing company on the African continent, with a near-total market share in the southern part of the continent. This includes all the Lion and Castle brands, as well as license-brewed Heineken and Amstel.

In Nigeria, the familiar Star Brand is brewed by the Nigerian Brewery, Ltd, a joint venture founded in November 1946 by the British United Africa Company (UAC) and Heineken of the Netherlands. The brewery,

ABOVE: South African Breweries (SAB) brands include the famous independent names that merged to form SAB in 1956, including Ohlsson's Cape Breweries, Ohlsson's Lion brand and that of the old Castle Brewery. RIGHT: The Nigerian Breweries plant at Lagos.

which also brews the Heineken flagship brand, expanded in the 1960s, building plants in Chad, Ghana and Sierra Leone.

The first brewery in the Nigerian capital of Lagos was the flagship plant of Nigerian Breweries, which opened in 1949 as the first bottle of Star Lager rolled off the bottling plant line. Additional breweries were added at Aba in 1957, Kaduna in 1963 and Ibadan in 1982 as production grew steadily.

Another of West Africa's most important brewing companies is Golden Guinea, located in Umuahia, Nigeria. Golden Guinea was founded in 1962 as the Independence Brewery Ltd—by then known as the Eastern Nigeria Development Corporation—the investment arm of the government of the former Easter Region of Nigeria. Golden Guinea Lager was launched into the Nigerian market the following year. The company began producing its second product, Eagle Stout, in 1967, thereby becoming one of the two breweries producing stout in the country at that time. In 1971, the company changed its name to Golden Guinea Breweries, Ltd. As a result of the reconstitution of the country into states, the ownership of Golden Guinea Breweries, Ltd passed to the East Central State government and on to the Imo State government in 1976. Today, Golden Guinea receives technical assistance from Holsten Bräuerei AG of Hamburg in the areas of improved production processes and equipment, raw materials research, quality assurance and marketing. In 1992 Bergedorf

BELOW: A selection of African lager brands including Kenya's Tusker; two brands from Nigeria's Golden Guinea; Gambia's (Ban)JulBrew; the Congo's Ngok and two from the island nation of Mauritius. Phoenix is a consistent medal winner and Ngok is named from the phonetic spelling of Le Choc (crocodile).

Malta was launched into the Nigerian market.

Another West African brewing concern under German management is the Banjul Breweries, Ltd in Banjul, Gambia, which is managed by Bräuhaase International of Hamburg. Banjul's flagship brand, JulBrew Lager, was awarded a gold medal in Luxembourg in 1990.

In East Africa, one of the key brewing companies is Kenya Breweries, Ltd of Nairobi, which brews Tusker, White Cap and Pilsner, all of which are lagers. Kenya Breweries had subsidiaries in both Uganda and Tanzania, and is affiliated with the Delta Corporation in Zimbabwe, a supplier of hops. In 1992, Kenya Breweries sold its interest in Seychelles Breweries, Ltd to Guinness International.

One of the largest European possessions in Africa during the colonial period was the Belgian Congo (now Zaire). With Belgium being the important brewing nation that it is, there is little wonder that brewing would take place in the Congo. It is only surprising insofar as the brewing industry there didn't really begin to roll until the 1920s. Among the important players in the industry were the Groupe Lambert (later Bruxelles Lambert) and Interbra. The Brasserie de Leopoldville was opened in the city of that name in 1923 and became Bralima in 1957. Nationalized by the Zaire government in 1975, Bralima struggled for a decade before the government allowed part of the seized shares to be returned to Bralima's former shareholders, including both Bruxelles Lambert and Heineken.

In the Republic of the Congo, the SCBK Brewery at Pointe Noire near Brazzaville (formerly Stanleyville) brews a beer known as *Ngok*, the phonetic spelling of *Le Choc*, which means 'crocodile.' The Ngok was the symbol of the pre-colonial Ki-Kongo region of equatorial Africa, but the beer is a lager rather than a pre-colonial style. Meanwhile, Solibra Brewery brews Mamba, an export lager, at its facility at Abidjan, the capital of the Ivory Coast.

The Mauritius Brewery, located on the island of the same name, has brewed Phoenix Lager Beer, a pilsener type, since 1963. Phoenix won the Gold Medal at Brewex in 1983 and the Gold Medal at Monde Sélection in 1989. Stella Lager Beer, brewed since 1964, won a Gold Medal at Brewex in 1976 and at the Monde Sélection in 1981 and 1989. Blue Marlin Lager Beer has been brewed and bottled since 1989 and won a Gold Medal at the Monde Sélection in 1992. The brewery has brewed and bottled Guinness under license since 1975.

During the nineteenth century, German and British breweries were opened in Egypt and the Middle East, just as the French were developing the sunny hills of Morocco, Algeria and Tunisia for viticulture. As with the European lands on the north side of the Mediterranean, beer drinking was never too widespread in this region, except among British and German expatriates, who were numerous until the mid-twentieth century and the rise of nationalism.

In Egypt, there were two notable European breweries, Bières Bomonti & Pyramides in Cairo and the Crown Brewery in Alexandria. After World War I, they jointly marketed a mass-market Pilsen-style lager known as Stella (Star). During World War II, while breweries in Europe suffered or closed, production of Stella increased sixfold because of the huge number of Allied

MAJOR BREWERIES OF AFRICA AND THE MIDDLE EAST

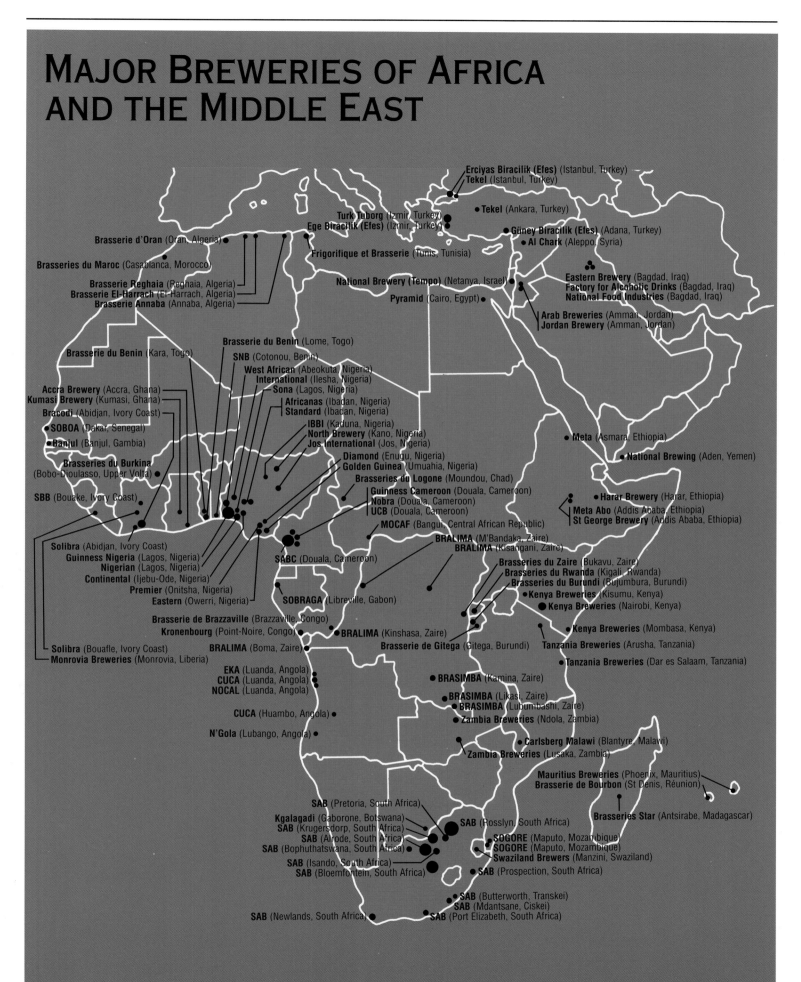

Erciyas Biracilik (Efes) (Istanbul, Turkey)
Tekel (Istanbul, Turkey)

Tekel (Ankara, Turkey)

Turk Tuborg (Izmir, Turkey)
Ege Biracilik (Efes) (Izmir, Turkey)

Güney Biracilik (Efes) (Adana, Turkey)
Al Chark (Aleppo, Syria)

Brasserie d'Oran (Oran, Algeria)

Frigorifique et Brasserie (Tunis, Tunisia)

Brasseries du Maroc (Casablanca, Morocco)

National Brewery (Tempo) (Netanya, Israel)

Eastern Brewery (Bagdad, Iraq)
Factory for Alcoholic Drinks (Bagdad, Iraq)
National Food Industries (Bagdad, Iraq)

Brasserie Reghaia (Reghaia, Algeria)
Brasserie El-Harrach (El-Harrach, Algeria)
Brasserie Annaba (Annaba, Algeria)

Pyramid (Cairo, Egypt)

Arab Breweries (Amman, Jordan)
Jordan Brewery (Amman, Jordan)

Brasserie du Benin (Lome, Togo)

Brasserie du Benin (Kara, Togo)

SNB (Cotonou, Benin)

West African (Abeokuta, Nigeria)
International (Ilesha, Nigeria)
Sona (Lagos, Nigeria)

Accra Brewery (Accra, Ghana)
Kumasi Brewery (Kumasi, Ghana)
Bracodi (Abidjan, Ivory Coast)

Africanas (Ibadan, Nigeria)
Standard (Ibadan, Nigeria)

SOBOA (Dakar, Senegal)

IBBI (Kaduna, Nigeria)
North Brewery (Kano, Nigeria)
Jos International (Jos, Nigeria)

Banjul (Banjul, Gambia)

Meta (Asmara, Ethiopia)

Diamond (Enugu, Nigeria)
Golden Guinea (Umuahia, Nigeria)

National Brewing (Aden, Yemen)

Brasseries du Burkina
(Bobo-Dioulasso, Upper Volta)

Brasseries du Logone (Moundou, Chad)

Guinness Cameroon (Douala, Cameroon)
Nobra (Douala, Cameroon)
UCB (Douala, Cameroon)

Harar Brewery (Harar, Ethiopia)
Meta Abo (Addis Ababa, Ethiopia)
St George Brewery (Addis Ababa, Ethiopia)

SBB (Bouake, Ivory Coast)

MOCAF (Bangui, Central African Republic)

BRALIMA (M'Bandaka, Zaire)
BRALIMA (Kisangani, Zaire)

Solibra (Abidjan, Ivory Coast)
Guinness Nigeria (Lagos, Nigeria)
Nigerian (Lagos, Nigeria)
Continental (Ijebu-Ode, Nigeria)
Premier (Onitsha, Nigeria)
Eastern (Owerri, Nigeria)

SABC (Douala, Cameroon)

Brasseries du Zaire (Bukavu, Zaire)
Brasseries du Rwanda (Kigali, Rwanda)
Brasseries du Burundi (Bujumbura, Burundi)
Kenya Breweries (Kisumu, Kenya)
Kenya Breweries (Nairobi, Kenya)

SOBRAGA (Libreville, Gabon)

Brasserie de Brazzaville (Brazzaville, Congo)
Kronenbourg (Point-Noire, Congo)

BRALIMA (Kinshasa, Zaire)

Brasserie de Gitega (Gitega, Burundi)

Kenya Breweries (Mombasa, Kenya)

Tanzania Breweries (Arusha, Tanzania)

Solibra (Bouafle, Ivory Coast)
Monrovia Breweries (Monrovia, Liberia)

BRALIMA (Boma, Zaire)

Tanzania Breweries (Dar es Salaam, Tanzania)

EKA (Luanda, Angola)
CUCA (Luanda, Angola)
NOCAL (Luanda, Angola)

BRASIMBA (Kamina, Zaire)

CUCA (Huambo, Angola)

BRASIMBA (Likasi, Zaire)
BRASIMBA (Lubumbashi, Zaire)
Zambia Breweries (Ndola, Zambia)

N'Gola (Lubango, Angola)

Carlsberg Malawi (Blantyre, Malawi)
Zambia Breweries (Lusaka, Zambia)

Mauritius Breweries (Phoenix, Mauritius)
Brasserie de Bourbon (St Denis, Réunion)

Brasseries Star (Antsirabe, Madagascar)

SAB (Pretoria, South Africa)
Kgalagadi (Gaborone, Botswana)
SAB (Krugersdorp, South Africa)
SAB (Alrode, South Africa)
SAB (Bophuthatswana, South Africa)

SAB (Rosslyn, South Africa)

SOGORE (Maputo, Mozambique)
SOGORE (Maputo, Mozambique)
Swaziland Brewers (Manzini, Swaziland)

SAB (Isando, South Africa)
SAB (Bloemfontein, South Africa)

SAB (Prospection, South Africa)

SAB (Butterworth, Transkei)
SAB (Mdantsane, Ciskei)

SAB (Newlands, South Africa)

SAB (Port Elizabeth, South Africa)

ABOVE: The extensive product line of Tempo, Israel's largest brewery, includes four beers as well as a line of soft drinks.

BELOW: The products of the Arab Breweries of Amman, Jordan, include both regular and non-alcoholic lagers in keeping with local tastes.

troops stationed in Egypt. After the war, Stella's unprecedented boom continued until 1949. Heineken, which had held a share of Bomonti & Pyramides since before the war, continued to play a role until the company was placed under state control in 1956, although Heineken's own products were not brewed in Egypt by B&P.

Since the 1970s, with the resurgence of fundamentalist Islam—which forbids the consumption of alcohol—many of the breweries that had thrived in the region, particularly those in Iran, have closed. Notable breweries in the Middle East today include Efes in Turkey, Al Chark in Syria, National in Israel and the Jordan Brewery in Amman, Jordan. The Jordan Brewery Company, Ltd was founded in 1955 by Sa'd Abujaber & Sons, a Jordanian group, and the Amstel Brewery (now part of the Heineken group) of Amsterdam. The company built its brewery at Zerka north of Amman. The first Jordan Amstel Beer was distributed to the market in October 1958, and in 1964, this beer was awarded the Gold Medal in Paris. In 1972, the company began draft beer sales in designated outlets. Corn and malt were then, and still are, regularly imported from Holland, Belgium and France, and Styrian hops were imported from Yugoslavia until 1976 when the brewery began using hop concentrate imported from Germany. In 1987, there was a merger with the General Investment Company, Ltd, and in September 1989 Arab Breweries Company, Ltd became allied with Jordan Brewery.

Accounting for a 90 percent market share, the largest brewer in Israel is Tempo Beer Industries, Ltd, with breweries in Holon, Migdal, Haemek, Netanya and Yeroham. Tempo's flagship brand is Maccabee, a premium lager, and other products include Gold Star and Malt Star, as well as Danish Tuborg and American Budweiser which are brewed under license, and various soft drinks.

Turkey's leading brewing company is Anadolu Industri (aka Group Efes Pilsen), whose first brewery, Erciyas Biracilik ve Malt Sanayii, was established in Istanbul in 1966 and began marketing its beers in 1969. Additional breweries were opened in Izmir in 1969, Adana in 1977 and Ege in 1989. The company also maintains a maltery at Afyon and a hop facility at Tarbes. The flagship lager Efes Pilsen is available not only in Turkey but is exported throughout the Middle East and Africa, as well as to Europe. Löwenbräu is also produced under license from the Munich brewer.

The second biggest brewer in Turkey is Türk Tuborg of Izmir, an affiliate of the Danish Tuborg (owned by Carlsberg). The remainder of the market is served by three state-owned breweries located in rural areas.

BELOW: This portfolio of Turkey's major brands includes products from Carlsberg's Turk Tuborg and Efes, which was founded at Istanbul in 1966.

ASIA AND THE PACIFIC

James Samuelson, in his nineteenth-century *History of Drink*, suggested that the people of China were well acquainted with and practiced the art of fermentation. He quotes from a book of Chinese poetry, written about 1116 BC:

'See the mighty cups of horn
Round their ranks in order borne!
It excites no conduct rude;
Surely blessings haste to greet
Lord of virtues so complete.'

Samuelson's views were confirmed by Morewood in his *Essays on the Inventions and Customs of the Ancients* in which he proves that the Chinese came to love ale: 'Under the government of the Emperor Yu, or Ta-yu (2207 BC), the making of ale, or wine, from

The beers of Asia: Enjoying Asahi in Japan (BELOW), and celebrating Singapore's Tiger (OPPOSITE).

rice was invented by an ingenious agriculturist name I-tye, and that, as the use of this liquor was likely to be attended with evil consequences, the emperor expressly forbid the manufacture or drinking of it under the severest penalties. He even renounced it himself, and dismissed his cupbearer, lest, as he said, the princes, his successors, might suffer their hearts to be effeminated with so delicious a beverage. This, however, had not the desired effect, for having once tasted it, the people could never afterwards entirely abstain from the bewitching draught.

'It was, even at a very early period, carried to such excess and consumed in such abundance that the Emperor Kya, the Nero of China, in 1836 BC ordered 3000 of his subjects to jump into a large lake which he had prepared and filled with it, while Chin-vang in 1120 BC thought it prudent to assemble the princes to suppress its manufacture, as it

was the source of infinite misfortune in his dominions. The cultivation of the vine has been known and practiced in China from the most remote period. Indeed, all the songs which remain of the early dynasties down to that of the Han dynasty, which began in 206 BC, confirm this opinion.'

As in modern Japan, contemporary brewing in China had its origins in the nineteenth century with the arrival of Europeans, such as the Germans who built a brewery at Tsingtao (now Qingdao). The beer which is brewed there still bears the most widely recognized label of any beer exported from China: Tsingtao Lager. Today, Asia is home to two-thirds of the earth's population but produces less beer in real terms and less beer per capita than any other continent, except Africa. The major exceptions are Japan and China, which between them produce 75 percent of all beer brewed in Asia. After Japan and China, South Korea and the Philippines are roughly tied for a distant third place. In Asia, as in Africa, there are local copies of European-style lagers produced in most countries, and there are still many indigenous native beers to be found in the more remote corners of the continent.

Japan, which is today the world's fourth largest brewing nation, did not have an indigenous beer style prior to the nineteenth century. Like so many other elements of Western culture, beer was introduced into Japan by Commodore Matthew Perry when he made his historic visit in 1853. After the Meiji Reformation of 1868, there were attempts to brew domestic beer in Japan, but the first successful commercial brewery was set up in 1869 at Yokohama by the American firm of Wiegand & Copeland. This brewery, later sold to Japanese interests, evolved into the Kirin Brewery Company, Ltd, which is today the largest brewing company in the

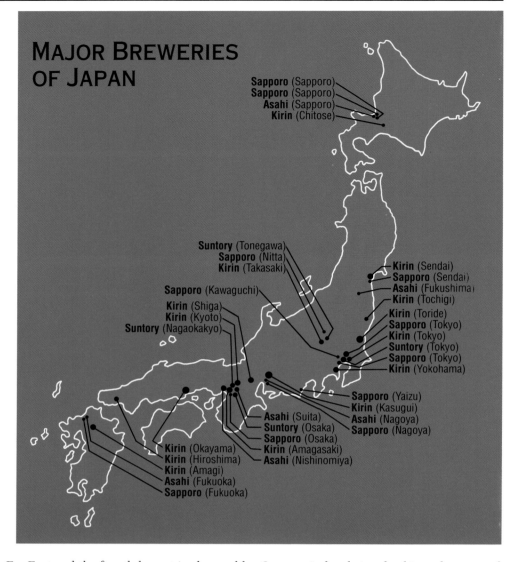

MAJOR BREWERIES OF JAPAN

Sapporo (Sapporo)
Sapporo (Sapporo)
Asahi (Sapporo)
Kirin (Chitose)

Suntory (Tonegawa)
Sapporo (Nitta)
Kirin (Takasaki)

Sapporo (Kawaguchi)
Kirin (Shiga)
Kirin (Kyoto)
Suntory (Nagaokakyo)

Kirin (Sendai)
Sapporo (Sendai)
Asahi (Fukushima)
Kirin (Tochigi)
Kirin (Toride)
Sapporo (Tokyo)
Kirin (Tokyo)
Suntory (Tokyo)
Sapporo (Tokyo)
Kirin (Yokohama)

Sapporo (Yaizu)
Kirin (Kasugui)
Asahi (Nagoya)
Sapporo (Nagoya)

Asahi (Suita)
Suntory (Osaka)
Sapporo (Osaka)
Kirin (Amagasaki)
Asahi (Nishinomiya)

Kirin (Okayama)
Kirin (Hiroshima)
Kirin (Amagi)
Asahi (Fukuoka)
Sapporo (Fukuoka)

Far East and the fourth largest in the world after Anheuser-Busch and Miller in the United States and Heineken of the Netherlands. Kirin exports to Europe and Asia, but Kirin beer for the North American market is brewed in Canada. Kirin labels used in the United States say 'imported' but the beer is imported from Canada, not Japan. Kirin currently maintains brewing facilities in Amagasaki (Osaka), Fukuoka, Hiroshima, Kyoto, Nagoya, Okayama, Sendai, Shiga, Takasaki, Tochigi, Tokyo, Toride and Yokohama.

In September 1993, Kirin entered into an agreement to produce the Anheuser-Busch flagship brand—Budweiser—under license for the Japanese market. Budweiser had actually been produced for the Japanese market since 1981 by Kirin's rival Suntory. However, the move to Kirin was seen as an opportunity to seize a much bigger market share for Bud, which was already the leading foreign brand in Japan.

The second of today's big Japanese brewers to be founded was Sapporo Breweries, Ltd, which was started in 1876 in the northern city of the same name that is seen as the mecca of Japanese brewing culture. As with other Japanese brewing companies,

Sapporo is deeply involved in real estate and leisure time activities, as well as in producing other beverages, including soft drinks and wines made with grapes from its own vineyards. Sapporo's product line now includes lagers, and a 'black' beer. Named for a good luck deity, Yebisu was first introduced in 1987. Sapporo describes this highly regarded beer as a 'stout draft,' although it is neither a stout nor a draft. Because Kirin brews in Canada, Sapporo is the leading Japanese import in the North American beer market.

In 1923, Shinjiro Torii built the first whiskey distillery in Japan at Yamazaki near Kyoto, thus founding the Japanese whiskey industry. His company, Suntory, was founded in 1899 with the intention of developing *wine* for export, and beer was not added to the Suntory product line until 1963. Suntory is really more of a vastly diversified real estate/leisure services company than a beverage producer. Nevertheless, Suntory, along with Asahi, is among Japan's top four brewing companies.

Founded in its present form in 1949, Asahi Breweries produces a variety of lagers for the domestic and export markets, including Edomae Draft and Asahi Z, as well as Asahi

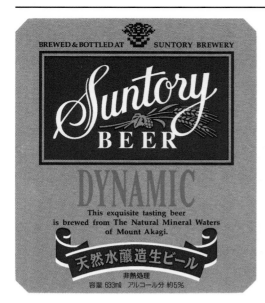

ABOVE: Suntory pulls no punches in celebrating this particular lager. RIGHT: Suntory's big brewing plant at Tonegawa opened in 1982.

FACING PAGE: Leading brands from Japan's big two, Kirin and Sapporo. Kirin is named for the mythical beast of Chinese folklore, Sapporo for Japan's leading brewing city.

BELOW: Asahi's product line includes its own ale, as well as foreign brands brewed under license from the USA, Germany, Australia, Britain and New Zealand.

MAJOR BREWERIES OF ASIA AND THE PACIFIC

● Haerbin Brewery (Haerbin, China)

Shenyang Brewery (Shenyang, China) ●

Guoying Brewery (Beijing, China) ●
Wuxing Brewery (Beijing, China) ●

● Chosun (Seoul, South Korea)
● Oriental (OB) (Seoul, South Korea)

Tianjin Brewery (Tianjin, China) ●

Muree (Rawalpindi, Pakistan) ●

Tsingtao Brewery (Qingdao, China)
● Shanghai Brewery (Shanghai, China)

● Mohan Meakin (Solan) (Solan, India)

Wuhan Brewery (Wuhan, China)

Mohan Nagar (Ghaziabad, India) ●

● Nepal Brewery (Kathmandu, Nepal)

● Taiwan Tobacco & Wine (Taipei, Taiwan)

Huizhou Brewing (Huizhou City, China)
● Carlsberg Hong Kong (Hong Kong, China)
San Miguel (Hong Kong, China)
Hong Kong Brewery (Hong Kong, China)

Kalyani (Calcutta, India) ●

Mandalay Brewery (Mandalay, Burma)

● Asia (Manila, Philippines)
● San Miguel (Manila, Philippines)

Mohan Rocky Springwater (Khopoli, India) ●

United (Bangalore, India) ●

● Boon Rawd (Bangkok, Thailand)
● Thai Amarit (Bangkok, Thailand)

● I'Indochine (Saigon, Viet Nam)

Ceylon (Nuwara Eliya, Sri Lanka) ●
McCallum (Colombo, Sri Lanka) ●

Multi Bintang (Medan, Indonesia) ●
Malayan (Kuala Lumpur, Malaysia) ●
Carlsberg Malaysia (Kuala Lumpur, Malaysia) ●

● Guinness Malaysia (Petaling Jaya, Malaysia)
● Asia Pacific (Singapore)

Multi Bintang (Tangerang, Indonesia) ●
● Delta Djakarta (Jakarta, Indonesia)
● Multi Bintang (Surabaya, Indonesia)

Rimba Subur (Bogor, Indonesia)
San Miguel (Tambun, Indonesia)

See page 30 for map of Japan.

FACING PAGE: Two of the most widely recognized lagers from northern Asia are China's Tsingtao and South Korea's OB, brewed by the Oriental Brewery in Seoul. BELOW, FROM TOP: Leading brands from India, the Philippines and Hong Kong. RIGHT: Known for its flagship Tiger Beer, Asia Pacific of Singapore also brews Anchor Lager.

Original Ale. Asahi also distributes or brews various foreign beers under license, including Coors from the United States, Löwenbräu from Germany, Bass from England, Fosters from Australia and Steinlager from New Zealand.

The largest and best known brand and brewing company in the Philippines was also the first brewing company in Southeast Asia. Don Enrique Barretto de Ycaza founded his La Fabrica de Cerveza de San Miguel in 1890, eight years before the Spanish relinquished control of the Philippines to the United States in the Spanish-American War.

Korea's largest brewing company is the Oriental Brewery Company, Ltd in Seoul, which markets OB Lager.

Among the leading brewing companies in India are Kalyani Breweries (Calcutta), the Mohan Nagar Brewery (Uttar Pradesh) and the Solan Brewery (Mimachal Pradesh). Mohan Meakin, Ltd, which owns Mohan Nagar, was founded in 1855. Taj Mahal is a popular export brand, while Golden Eagle is the largest selling brand in India.

Malayan Breweries, Ltd (MBL) was formed in Singapore in 1930 as a joint venture between the Fraser & Neave Group of Companies (F&N) and Heineken NV of Holland. In 1946, writer Anthony Burgess, while searching for a title for his book about life in Malaysia and Singapore, obtained permission to use the then advertising slogan for their Tiger Beer, 'Time for a Tiger.' Now known as Asia Pacific Breweries (APB), the company produces a line of lagers and stouts—led by Tiger Beer, of course.

During 1992 and 1993, APB introduced two new lagers, Tiger Classic, a seasonal beer released during the Lunar New Year celebration, and Raffles Light, named for Singapore's legendary hotel which was literally the crossroads of an empire for decades. At the end of 1993, APB opened a new brewing plant in Ho Chi Minh City (Saigon) in partnership with Vietnamese interests. In addition to cooperative efforts with Guinness of Ireland and Heineken of the Netherlands, APB also distributes South Pacific Lager, brewed in Papua New Guinea, and St Louis Pêche, a peach lambic from Belgium.

AUSTRALIA
AND
NEW ZEALAND

Although they do not rank among the world's largest brewing nations, both of the English-speaking island nations of the southwest Pacific rank high in per capita enjoyment of our favorite beverage. Then, too, the Elders IXL Group, which is the parent of Australia's Carlton & United Brewers (CUB)—as well as Courage in the UK—is one of the four largest brewing companies in the world. Today, the two largest Australian brewing companies are Elders IXL, whose flagship brand is the ubiquitous Foster's Lager, and Lion Nathan, which owns

numerous formerly independent brewers, including Castlemaine Perkins, Swan in Perth and Toohey's, with breweries in New South Wales, as well as several brewers in New Zealand. One of Australia's most important independents, and the leading ale brewer in the land, is Cooper's, founded in South Australia in 1862.

Although beer had arrived in Australia on ships from Britain as early as 1788, it was a settler named John Boston who was the first to actually *make* commercial beer in Australia. In 1796, he used malted maize and Cape

gooseberries, as he, like his successors, not only had to cope with the country's hot climate and lack of good quality ingredients, but also with the problem that the beer deteriorated when it was transported long distances to market.

Today, the most common type of beer in Australia is lager, but unlike the rest of the world, lager did not make an impact on production until the 1880s. The hot weather encouraged beer drinking, but it also played havoc with yeast. Ales were made, although in most cases, not very well. 'Tasteless, insipid and sugary' was the verdict on locally made beer in the early days of colonial settlement.

Castlemaine Perkins originated with Nicholas and Edward Fitzgerald, the sons of Francis Fitzgerald, a well-known Irish brewer. The brothers first came to Australia in the 1850s and established the Castlemaine Brewery in Castlemaine, Victoria. The Castlemaine township was named after a small village in Ireland, where a castle stood on the banks of the Maine River—hence the name. Evidently the township came into existence quite rapidly during a gold strike in 1853. The Fitzgerald brothers quickly extended their activities to Melbourne, Sydney, Newcastle, Adelaide, Perth and Brisbane. It was in Brisbane that they formed the partnership with Quinlan Gray & Company and a Sydney brewer, Robert Predergast. The association with Predergast was an exten-

LEFT: The distinctive home of Tasmania's Cascade Brewery was completed in 1927. FACING PAGE: The Toohey family first brewed beer in 1865.

sion of their interests in establishing a brewery in Newcastle, New South Wales, in 1876.

The first brew produced by the new Milton brewery was made to the same formula as the beer brewed by Castlemaine Brewery in Victoria. It was called Castlemaine XXX Sparkling Ale, and was ready for sale on Friday, 13 September 1878. The *Brisbane Courier* described the new brew as a 'delicious ale of the brightest amber, pleasant to taste, with a peculiarity of flavor not easily described, and an aroma of an appetizing nature by itself.' The prophetic journalist also wrote, 'If Messrs Fitzgerald Quinlan and Company provide the public from one year's end to the other with such a beverage, they will have no reason to repent their venture in the Colony.'

Although a 'Castlemaine (XXXX) Sparkling Prize Ale' had been produced at Milton from the early 1880s—indeed, it won a 'Special Prize' at the First International Exhibition in Sydney in 1883—it was not until the financial crash of the early 1880s that the brewery applied for the first trademark showing four Xs. Until this time, the brewery had been producing Milton Beer and also Castlemaine (XXX) Sparkling Ale. The trademark for the new XXXX brew showed an eagle carrying a barrel with XXXX written on it. The beer was simply called Castlemaine Sparkling Ale. The four Xs were still

quite low in profile at this time. The Xs were chosen because, since medieval times, when brewing was confined mainly to monasteries, X—the sign of the cross—had been a standard symbol of purity for alcoholic beverages. The number of Xs represents the strength of the beer.

In 1924, the now familiar XXXX Bitter Ale became available for sale. Bill Leitner, the company's head brewer, imported yeast cultures from Europe and experimented to produce the right type of beer. XXXX Bitter Ale proved to be the most popular, and it was this formula that became the basis for the modern product. In February 1924, the first advertisement for XXXX Bitter Ale appeared in the *Brisbane Courier*. In October of that year, the first caricature of 'Mr Fourex' appeared. This advertisement called the beer 'Fourex.' A month later another Mr Fourex ad appeared, this time with a hat emblazoned with four Xs.

Over the years there has been much speculation as to just who the little Mr Fourex was. Some say he was actually Paddy Fitzgerald, who was the general manager of Castlemaine Perkins Brewery during a period of great growth. There certainly seems to be a degree of similarity. However, the little man was on the scene long before Paddy became a moving force in Milton. Others have hypothesized that Mr Fourex

THIS PAGE: The Castlemaine Perkins product line contains many brews, but none so notable as the ubiquitous XXXX. Even the XL brand, which is now part of the Castlemaine Perkins family, is the Roman numeral equivalent. Applied to everything from ale to lager, the XXXX brand has been around since the 1880s, although the accompanying cartoon character, Mr Fourex (BELOW), made his appearance in 1924.

was modeled on a well-known dwarf who sold newspapers in Fortitude Valley in the 1930s. At Castlemaine Perkins they like to believe that Mr Fourex is a product of the era in which XXXX was born, as other advertising goods of the day show similar-looking figures. None of these have, however have achieved the longevity, popularity and community standing enjoyed by Mr Fourex, but then again, they never had XXXX to their credit.

One of the greatest milestones in the history of the company occurred in 1928 when negotiations were completed with Perkins & Company for the purchase of its Brisbane & Toowoomba Breweries and its Toowoomba Maltings. This deal also included the purchase of a number of freehold and leasehold hotels. Perkins & Company had a history almost as old as the Castlemaine Brewery partnership. Formed in 1881, for a long time it was one of the most prosperous breweries in Queensland, but fierce competition with XXXX during the 1920s had contributed to the fall in much of Perkins' trade. Comparatively speaking, Perkins & Company had started on a moderate scale. Brothers Paddy and Thomas Perkins had emigrated to Australia from Ireland in 1851. Their speculative diggings at Bendigo and Ballarat proved quite successful. In 1866, they gave up mining and started a brewery in Toowoomba, Queensland. In 1872, they bought the Brisbane City Brewery on Mary Street, which had been established in the early 1860s.

When Castlemaine Brewery took control in 1928, however, all operations at the Perkins' Brisbane Brewery ceased. The new company became known as Castlemaine Perkins, Ltd. A large part of their Mary Street brewery was destroyed by fire a few years later but malting and brewery operations continued at Toowoomba until 1958, when all of the company's operations were concentrated at Milton.

Castlemaine Bitter Ale was the major product manufactured by Castlemaine Perkins Brewery between 1924 and 1970. The sale of some Perkins products, such as Perkins XXX Ale, Sparkling Ale and Carbine, as well as Nurse & Gooley's Stout, did continue until 1934, but sales were extremely poor and most of these products were discontinued. Castlemaine Perkins continued to grow, as did the sales of XXXX Bitter Ale, until 1970 when it was decided to produce another beer product called XXXX Draught. Other additions to the Castlemaine brand followed, including XXXX Lite, DL (Diet lager), Castlemaine Gold and the limited draught production of Games Special during the 1982 Commonwealth Games in Brisbane.

In 1980, Castlemaine Perkins merged with Toohey's to form Castlemaine Toohey's. This merger gave the newly formed brewing group a strong hold on the Australian East Coast market, and in September 1983 it launched XXXX in New South Wales and Victoria, where it readily gained an excellent market share.

Overseas markets were also developed by Castlemaine Perkins, starting with the export of beer to Australian troops in the Middle East in 1941. Today, Castlemaine XXXX is exported to some 40 countries and has become one of the most recognized lagers in England.

Toohey's originated with Matthew and Honora Toohey, who emigrated from Ireland in 1841. They settled in rural Victoria to raise cattle, but they moved to Melbourne in 1860 to take up the license of the Limerick Arms Hotel in Emerald Hill. In 1865, on a visit to Sydney, their son John Thomas Toohey heard that the Darling Brewery was for sale and convinced his brother James

Matthew to join him in the business. Under the name JT and J Toohey, their company prospered, and after a few years they expanded to a larger site. Toohey's and the rival Tooth & Company rose to dominance in the 1880s with the popularity of their beers. They remained rivals for a century.

The differences between the two included religion—the Tooheys were Catholic while the Tooth family from England was Anglican. It was Tooth's, however, which dominated the market in New South Wales for most of the century by supplying their beer to a massive hotel network 'tied' to the brewery. Changes in liquor industry regulation from the mid-1950s helped Toohey's break this monopoly. The emergence of clubs and liquor shops allowed Toohey's to respond to the developments, while Tooth's retained their focus on hotels. Toohey's position was not sustained, and the revitalization of the

BELOW: Castlemaine's Milton brewery in Brisbane, Queensland, as it appeared in 1879.

old Tooth Brewery under the guidance of Carlton & United Breweries saw the latter wrest the laurels back from a struggling Toohey's in the 1980s. Eventually, Toohey's merged with Castlemaine Perkins in March 1980. Ownership of Toohey's shifted to the Bond Corporation in September 1985, and then to National Brewing Holdings in October 1990. Though not used on all products, the 'stag' logo has been part of the history of Toohey's since 1869. The stag can be traced to John Toohey's favorite hotel, the Bald Faced Stag Hotel in Leichhardt. The hotel opened in the 1830s and still stands in the same spot today. The head of a stag mounted on the bar wall caught Toohey's attention, and folklore holds that there and then he decided to use the stag as the symbol for the new brewery he was planning. When the brewery moved to Elizabeth Street in Sydney, the main brewery building had a large stag painted on a billboard atop the roof. When the family firm was incorporated at the turn of the century, the stag became the trademark. When the company moved to Auburn, the cornerstone of the building was a bas relief of a sitting stag.

Carlton & United Brewers (CUB), now part of the Elders IXL Group, has its roots in the old Carlton Brewery, born during the golden age of brewing in the 1850s at a time when the city of Melbourne had 35 breweries. Today CUB is a holding company with a history that spans more than a century and a half and includes 126 breweries. The flagship brand, Foster's, is ironically named for a pair of American brothers who spent only about 18 months in Australia. They founded their Foster Brewing Company in Melbourne in 1887, sold it the following year and went home, never to be heard from again.

Toohey's Bitter, as brewed at the Standard brewery (ABOVE LEFT) in the 1920s, is a classic today (ABOVE RIGHT). Toohey's also brewed a stout (BELOW).

The famous stag logo has graced all of the Toohey's products (FACING PAGE AND ABOVE) since it was borrowed from the Bald Faced Stag Hotel in Leichhardt in 1869.

ABOVE: Boag's beers are brewed in Tasmania by Cascade. BELOW: The Carlton & United (CUB) portfolio is extensive, but the flagship is Foster's Lager. RIGHT: The Swan Brewery near Perth (which also brews Emu) joined the flock of Lion Nathan in 1992.

When CUB was formed as a multi-company consortium in 1907, Carlton was the largest partner, followed by McCracken's, Victoria and Castlemaine, with Shamrock and Foster's being the two smallest components.

Foster's quickly grew in importance within CUB, and by 1937 posters were already declaring it 'Australia's National Beverage.' Fifty years later, Australian film personality Paul Hogan, a Foster's spokesman, declared that 'Foster's is Australian for "beer," mate!'

Far from the more populous metropolitan areas in New South Wales and Victoria, Western Australia got its first brewery—James Stokes' Albion Brewery—in Perth in 1837. The Swan Brewery, which was to become the brewer of Australia's second most identifiable lager brand, originated with Frederick Sherwood, who began brewing in Perth in 1857. Captain John Maxwell Ferguson and William Mumme of the Stanley Brewing Company, leased the Swan

Brewery in 1874, and around 1887 acquired the Lion Brewery. In 1908, the name of the Stanley Brewery was changed to Emu Brewery, and in 1928, Swan purchased Emu.

In 1978, Swan moved from Perth to a large, modern new brewery constructed at Canning Vale, Western Australia. In 1982, Swan became a wholly owned subsidiary of Bond Corporation Holdings, Ltd, and in 1985, Bond purchased Castlemaine Toohey's, Ltd, and by 1987, The Swan Brewery Company, Toohey's and Castlemaine Perkins, together with the Pittsburgh Brewing Company of Pennsylvania and G Heileman Brewing Company of the United States, made up the Bond Brewing Group of Companies. However, in 1990, Swan, together with Toohey's and Castlemaine Perkins, were purchased by National Brewing Holdings, a joint venture partnership between Bell Resources (now Australian Consolidated Investments) and Lion Nathan. The Swan Brewery Company became a wholly owned subsidiary of Lion Nathan Australia in 1992. The Swan product line includes those represented by the sign of the graceful swan, as well as those of the flightless emu, a bird native to Australia.

The Cascade Brewery Company, Ltd was incorporated in 1883 in Tasmania, the island state off the tip of Victoria. A soft drink and bottled water plant was installed in 1885 and in 1922 the company acquired J Boag & Son, brewers of Boag's beer at Launceston. The following year, the company entered the wine and spirit business, and for a time, the grocery business. In 1981, Industrial Equity, Ltd (IEL) succeeded in gaining more than 50 percent of Cascade and purchased the remaining shares in 1985. Following the market crash of October 1987, IEL sold Cascade to Wilson Neil Australia, whose name was changed to the Cascade Group in 1988. Cascade's Razor Edge Lager was developed for the American market with a label featuring fauna more common to northern Australia than Tasmania.

Based in Thebarton near Adelaide, the South Australian Brewing Company was formed in 1888 by the merger of Kent Town Brewery, the West End Brewery and a wine and spirit merchant. The principle figures in the merger were William Simms, who had started the West End Brewery in 1859, Sir Edwin Smith, owner of the Kent Town Brewery, and Robert Stock. Stock, who had been Smith's manager at Kent Town, became the first chairman of South Australian Brewing, and it was he who masterminded the successful joint venture. The first head brewmaster for the new company was George William Bone. Soon, other small breweries were acquired in Broken Hill, Waverly and Port Augusta. Several of these were eventually closed, but their distribution channels were an asset.

BELOW AND RIGHT: South Australian Brewing near Adelaide blends modern mechanization with a tradition that includes the legacy of many colorful brand names.

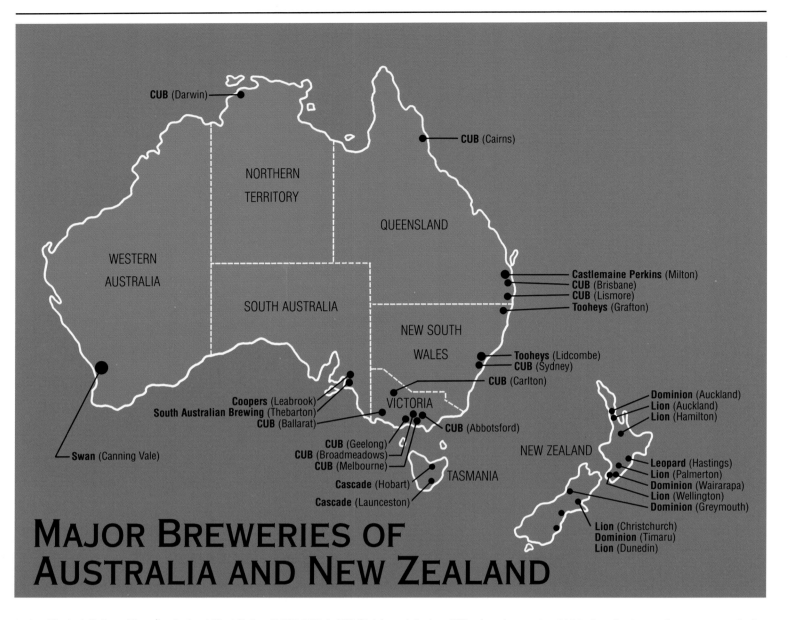

MAJOR BREWERIES OF AUSTRALIA AND NEW ZEALAND

Map labels:
- CUB (Darwin)
- CUB (Cairns)
- NORTHERN TERRITORY
- QUEENSLAND
- WESTERN AUSTRALIA
- SOUTH AUSTRALIA
- NEW SOUTH WALES
- Castlemaine Perkins (Milton)
- CUB (Brisbane)
- CUB (Lismore)
- Tooheys (Grafton)
- Tooheys (Lidcombe)
- CUB (Sydney)
- CUB (Carlton)
- Coopers (Leabrook)
- South Australian Brewing (Thebarton)
- CUB (Ballarat)
- VICTORIA
- CUB (Abbotsford)
- Swan (Canning Vale)
- CUB (Geelong)
- CUB (Broadmeadows)
- CUB (Melbourne)
- Cascade (Hobart)
- Cascade (Launceston)
- TASMANIA
- NEW ZEALAND
- Dominion (Auckland)
- Lion (Auckland)
- Lion (Hamilton)
- Leopard (Hastings)
- Lion (Palmerton)
- Dominion (Wairarapa)
- Lion (Wellington)
- Dominion (Greymouth)
- Lion (Christchurch)
- Dominion (Timaru)
- Lion (Dunedin)

BELOW: The installation of lagering tanks at West End Brewery in 1906. Australians pursued the turn-of-the-century fad of giving German names to many lagers.

FACING PAGE: In 1991, Steinlager introduced 'Blue,' reminiscent of Canada's Labatt 'Blue.' It is promoted by actors portraying the 'Blues Brothers.'

In 1938 South Australian acquired the Walkerville Brewing Company (renamed the Southwark Brewery), which had been established in 1886 as the Torrenside Brewery. By 1915, Walkerville had become the leading brewer in South Australia with over half of the market, while South Australian's West End plant held less than one-third of the market. Gradually, these positions changed after the Great Depression struck the Australian economy and merger discussions began in the early 1930s.

During World War II, production held steady owing to the Control of Liquor Order, which limited domestic distribution to two-thirds of the prewar level in order to divert beer to the armed forces. The postwar years were successful ones, highlighted by a brief association with Guinness of Ireland in the 1960s wherein Guinness Stout was brewed at South Australian's Southwark Brewery. South Australian also made a cooperative agreement with Cooper & Sons, which by the 1960s was the only other brewing company in South Australia. This agreement assured the survival of Cooper's—which was an ale brewer rather than a lager brewer like South Australian—as an independent company.

Brewing ceased at Kent Town in the early years of the twentieth century but continued at West End Brewery until 1980. Today, all brewing is done at the Southwark Brewery in Thebarton, one of the most technologically advanced brewing complexes in the world.

South Australian still uses the names of the former brewing plants for its products. The West End family of lagers includes Premium, Draught, Light Export and Export Dry. The Southwark family includes Bitter, Premium, Special, Gold and Old Southwark Stout. There is also a family known as Eagle, presumably for Adelaide's famous hotel that once sold a wide range of West End—as well as Walkerville and Cooper's—beers. The product line is completed by Kent Town Ale and a draught product named for the old Broken Hill Brewery, which was originally acquired in 1889.

Probably the most well-known New Zealand beer on the international market is Steinlager, which is brewed in Auckland by Lion Breweries in Auckland. The company dates to the brewery originally built by Richard Secombe at the corner of Mountain Road and Khyber Pass Road in Aukland in 1859. Today, the company is owned by Australia's Lion Nathan Group. Along with Steinlager, Lion brews Rheinbeck, Waikato Bitter and Lion Red. In 1991, Lion introduced Steinlager Blue, a variation on the original Steinlager concept, which was marketed with an advertising campaign featuring characters based on the American film *The Blues Brothers*.

On New Zealand's South Island, the leading brewer is New Zealand Breweries, which has plants in both Christchurch and Dunedin and is associated with Lion on the North Island. The company dates to the Crown Brewery, which was established in Christchurch in the 1850s. Famous for its India Pale Ale, Crown became the cornerstone of New Zealand Breweries when it was formed in 1923. Current brands include Speight's, Speight's Extra Gold and Canterbury Draught. The company also brews Guinness Stout under license from Guinness in Dublin, Ireland.

Managed as a separate business unit is the central region of New Zealand Breweries based in Wellington, with a brewery in Hastings in the Hawkes Bay area. Products brewed here include Lion Brown—the region's biggest-selling beer—Red Band, a 'boutique brand' originally introduced in Wellington in response to the microbrewery trend and Hawkes Bay Draught, which was introduced in 1991.

BELGIUM

In the world of beer and brewing, Belgium is a place apart. There is as large a range of beer styles in this small country as there is in all the rest of the world, and Belgium has more breweries per capita than any other nation on earth. When the Belgian brewing industry bills the nation as a 'Beer Paradise,' it may actually be making an understatement. The vast spectrum of beer styles ranges from mass-market lagers, to fruit beers fermented with wild yeast, to rich, dark ales from breweries run by Trappist monks, to the exciting beers of the smaller, newer breweries.

When it comes to Belgian beer, all of the superlatives apply. While absolute volume and per capita consumption are less, Belgian beer drinkers can make their choices from a dizzying variety and level of quality unheard of elsewhere. Until the North American microbrewery revolution, there were more brewing companies in Belgium than in the entire Western Hemisphere. These breweries range from those brewing the hugely popular Jupiler and Stella Artois brands, to tiny firms the size of North American microbreweries, that have remained small for years, or even centuries.

In the region that is now modern Belgium, beer was first brewed on private farms. Until the eleventh century, commercial beer was the prerogative of the abbeys, over a dozen of which are still brewing commercial quantities of beer. Later, brewing became a trade and brewers formed influential guilds to protect not only the producers, but their customers. The superb seventeenth-century guild houses of Belgian brewers, which still stand on the spectacular Grand Place in Brussels, bear witness to the importance and wealth of the Belgian brewing industry.

Brewing in Belgium is still largely the work of skilled artisans. At the turn of the century, there were more than 3000 brewers. Indeed, at one time, Belgium even had more brewers than burgermeisters. Only 150 breweries remain active today, but many of them have gained international recognition. Even though production equipment has been modernized, brewing techniques and regional recipes remain much the same as they were five centuries ago.

Today Belgium's two largest brewers—Jupiler and Stella Artois—are both part of the Interbrew Group. Founded in Jupille near Liège, the Jupiler Brewery dates back to 1853, while Artois in Leuven traces its roots to 1399.

Jupille is reputedly the birthplace of Charlemagne, with a history of brewing dating back to 1256. The Piedboeuf family, who founded Jupiler in 1853, has been in Jupille since 1445. Launched in 1966, Jupiler Lager from Jupille is Belgium's largest selling brand. Interbrew is investing a great deal of money in the expansion of the Jupiler plant.

The Artois Brewery dates to the House of Den Horen, an inn in Leuven which first brewed its own beer in 1366, and from 1537 sold its products to the University of Leuven

LEFT: The brewmaster carefully loads hops into the wort in a big copper kettle at the Artois brewery in Leuven.
FACING PAGE: A la Morte Subite in Brussels is one of the world's legendary beer halls.

(founded in 1425). Den Horen had many owners before Sebastien Artois bought it in 1717. He had been an apprentice there, earning the title of master brewer in 1708, and his many descendants included several master brewers. It was his grandson, Leonard, who managed a vigorous expansion, buying two neighboring breweries on the quays of the 'new' Leuven-Rupel Canal: the Fransche Kroon in 1787 and the Prins Karel in 1793. The Den Horen Artois brewery quickly became one of the largest in the Austro-Hungarian Empire, brewing some 63,000 barrels (71,000 hectoliters) per year. The Artois 'bock' beer was launched in 1892. It was a low-fermentation Pilsen-style lager that was the father of today's Stella Artois. Artois Brewery Company was incorporated in 1901, and soon after, Professor Verhelst, director of the Academy of Brewing at Leuven University, became its managing director and played a key role in its development and survival through two world wars. Stella Artois—literally the 'star of Artois'—was named after the Christmas star and was a 'special occasion' beer launched in 1926. Loburg was launched in 1977 as a 'premium' variation on Stella Artois Lager.

The Haacht Brewery, established in 1898, is the third largest brewer in Belgium. The company's main product is a Pilsner-style beer, called Primus in honor of Jan Primus I

FACING PAGE: The lagers Stella Artois and Jupiler, represent Belgium's two largest brewing companies, which are now part of the Leuven-based Interbrew Group. A lager brewed in Brussels, Loburg was introduced in 1977 as the premium counterpart to Stella Artois.

TOP AND ABOVE: Primus and Adler are among the principal lagers brewed by Haacht, Belgium's third largest brewer after Jupiler, Artois and Maes. RIGHT: The brewmaster at Haacht's brewhouse in Moortmeerbeek carefully tends the wort.

(Gambrinus), the duke of Brabant (1252-1294). Haacht also brews a large range of top-fermented beers such as Witbier Haacht, and two abbey-style beers. Haacht also brews regional beers such as Gildenbier and Charles Quint. Adler is a Dortmunder-type lager.

There are also still many small brewers in towns and villages across Belgium that date from various milestones across those five centuries. Adriaan Geerkens began brewing at his inn at Bocholt in 1758. His grand-daughter Isabella married Theodorus Martens in 1823 and their son Frans was an important factor in developing what would evolve into today's Martens Brewery. Still family-owned, the brewery went through a great expansion after World War II, and today exports both top- and bottom-fermented beer throughout Europe and the world. The Sezuens (Seasons) ale—on whose label winter hands a beer to summer—was awarded the Gold Medal of the World Beer Selection of Brussels in 1991.

In the nineteenth century, the large farms in the Hainault region grew barley and hops, and the village of Silly, situated here, has had a brewery since 1850. Founded as Cense de la Tour, the Brasserie de Silly is now run by the fourth generation of the same family. Since 1947, the brewery became more important than farming, producing only top-fermented beers such as Grisette, Saison and Scotch. By 1950, the brewery owned a number of cafés and had added the production of pils (a bottom-fermented beer) to its brands. In 1975, Silly acquired the Tennstedt Decroes Brewery at Enghien, which allowed Silly to add Double Enghien to its range. In 1990, Titje, a Brabantine-style blanche or witbier, was created. Another of Belgium's smaller brewers is St Feuillien in Le Roeulx, named for the saint who was martyred nearby in the sixth century. St Feuillien beer was brewed by the monks of the Abbaye de St Feuillien from 1125, but brewing has been in the non-monastic hands of the Friart family since 1873.

Placide Louwaege stopped farming in 1877 and moved to Kortemark to buy one of the five breweries then in existence, where he began to brew a lager called Akila (from the Latin 'aquila,' meaning eagle). In the meantime, the Louwaege family was also coming into its own, and Alfons, and later on Willy Louwaege, held the mayor's office in Kortemark for more than half a century. The

RIGHT FROM TOP: The lagers of Martens and Louwaege; and the top fermented beers of Brasserie de Silly. The latter includes 'Scotch' a popular local style in Belgium. FACING PAGE: St Feuillien's ales are not widely available in every size seen here.

present managing director, Jackie Louwaege, produces a new regional beer called Hapkin. It is a pale, top-fermented beer, whose recipe is said to have been invented in the Middle Ages by the fathers of the Abbey of Ter Duinen, at the request of the then Count of Flanders, Hapkin-with-the-Axe.

In 1880, the birth of a son inspired a man named De Splenter to set up a brewery. By the period between the two world wars, the De Splenter Brewery was regularly brewing some 50 barrels (60 hectoliters) of ale a week. In 1968, Yvan De Splenter renamed the enterprise Brouwerij Riva and built an ultramodern brewery.

By 1980, Riva ales were already being exported, mainly to Europe, but also to North America. Riva's holding company has recently acquired three regional 'house-breweries': Straffe Hendrik, Gouden Carolus and the noted lambic brewer, Liefmans.

Vondel Ale is named for Joost van den Vondel, the most famous Dutch writer of the Netherlands' Golden Age. Lucifer, named

after Vondel's best-known work, is a fiery, intense ale.

Alexander Rodenbach first began brewing at Roeselare in the province of West Flanders in 1836. The uniquely fruity Rodenbach ales are among the only beers in the world still aged in wooden tuns as pictured on the Grand Cru label. 'It was in 1880 that Egide Maes (pronounced *marse*) purchased the St Michael Brewery in Waarloos and began brewing the popular Pilsen-style lager that bears his name.

In a nation where many of the most notable ales are brewed by monks, perhaps the most well-known *secular* Belgian ale, is the famous Duvel, brewed by the Moortgat family at Breendonk. The brewery was founded in 1871 by Jan Leonart Moortgat, and under the second generation of brewers, Victor and Albert, the brewery started to develop new products, including a Brabant witbier call Steendonk. Today Moortgat also brews several Pilsen-style lagers: Bel, Godefroy, Silver and Wander.

ABOVE: Straffe Hendrik is a Flemish lager from Brugge, while Lucifer is a particularly fruity ale brewed by Riva in Dentergems (also in Flanders), who are better known for their witbier. RIGHT: Maes brews the third most popular lager in Belgium. BELOW: Rodenbach's ales, especially Grand Cru, are tart and distinct in their flavor. BOTTOM ROW AND FACING PAGE: The beers of the Moortgat Brewery in Breendonk, near Mechelen include Duvel (Devil), an extraordinary, strong but well-balanced, mildly fruity ale.

Brassée à l'eau de source

There are also several important microbreweries that opened a century after the likes of Maes and Louwaege opened their firms. La Chouffe in Achouffe near Bastogne in the Ardennes highlands was founded in 1982 by homebrewers Pierre Gobron and Christian Bauweraerts. The labels feature the *chouffe*, the legendary mute gnomes who found that drinking the water of the River Decrogne gave them the ability to speak. According to Gobron and Bauweraerts, they leave the raw materials for their beer in their brewhouse overnight and the chouffes do all the brewing.

De Dolle is a microbrewery that opened in Essen in 1980 with whimsical labels that are highly prized by collectors. Oerbier is the principal product, with a profoundly fruity, almost licorice aroma. Boskeun (Easter Bunny) is, as the name suggests, a seasonal beer. Different vintages have varying degrees of honey in the aroma, but all have hints of a Sauterne's sweetness. Arabier is a summer brew. The name represents an impossibly convoluted joke, but the beer is serious enough. Stille Nacht (Silent Night) is a Christmas beer with an especially high alcohol content of nine percent, a claret color and a fruity, apple-like aroma.

ABBEY BEERS

An important aspect of Belgian brewing is that of the abbey (*abbage* or *abdij*) beers, which are brewed by Trappist monks at monasteries throughout the country. Abbey ales, or Trappist ales as they are properly identified, are a recognized brewing style, and the ales are extremely popular, representing a dynamic line of continuity in the Belgian brewing heritage. For centuries monasteries were centers of literacy and study, art and science. Monasteries then evolved as brewing centers as well. They were also a refuge and resting place for pilgrims traveling to shrines or the Holy Land. Pilgrims who stayed for a night or two needed food and drink, so the monasteries brewed their own beer, made their own cheeses and baked bread, as some still do.

In much of Europe, the great era of monastic brewing came to an end when the abbeys were secularized by Napoleon or destroyed in the French Revolution. For the Belgian brewing industry, however, this was only a minor setback. After the revolution, religious orders from France crossed the border and built new abbeys. The monks were also

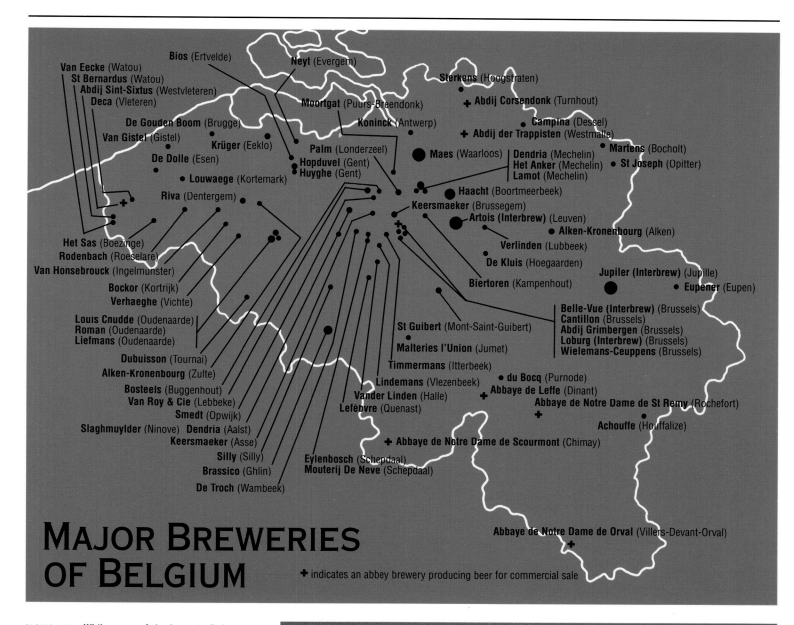

Bios (Ertvelde)
Neyt (Evergem)
Van Eecke (Watou)
St Bernardus (Watou)
Sterkens (Hoogstraten)
Abdij Sint-Sixtus (Westvleteren)
Deca (Vleteren)
Moortgat (Puurs-Breendonk)
Abdij Corsendonk (Turnhout)
De Gouden Boom (Brugge)
Koninck (Antwerp)
Campina (Dessel)
Van Gistel (Gistel)
Abdij der Trappisten (Westmalle)
Krüger (Eeklo)
Palm (Londerzeel)
Martens (Bocholt)
De Dolle (Esen)
Hopduvel (Gent)
Maes (Waarloos)
Dendria (Mechelin)
Huyghe (Gent)
Het Anker (Mechelin)
St Joseph (Opitter)
Louwaege (Kortemark)
Lamot (Mechelin)
Riva (Dentergem)
Haacht (Boortmeerbeek)
Keersmaeker (Brussegem)
Artois (Interbrew) (Leuven)
Alken-Kronenbourg (Alken)
Het Sas (Boezinge)
Verlinden (Lubbeek)
Rodenbach (Roeselare)
De Kluis (Hoegaarden)
Van Honsebrouck (Ingelmunster)
Jupiler (Interbrew) (Jupille)
Bockor (Kortrijk)
Biertoren (Kampenhout)
Eupener (Eupen)
Verhaeghe (Vichte)
Belle-Vue (Interbrew) (Brussels)
Louis Cnudde (Oudenaarde)
Cantillon (Brussels)
Roman (Oudenaarde)
St Guibert (Mont-Saint-Guibert)
Abdij Grimbergen (Brussels)
Liefmans (Oudenaarde)
Loburg (Interbrew) (Brussels)
Malteries l'Union (Jumet)
Wielemans-Ceuppens (Brussels)
Dubuisson (Tournai)
Alken-Kronenbourg (Zulte)
Timmermans (Itterbeek)
Bosteels (Buggenhout)
Lindemans (Vlezenbeek)
du Bocq (Purnode)
Van Roy & Cie (Lebbeke)
Vander Linden (Halle)
Abbaye de Leffe (Dinant)
Smedt (Opwijk)
Lefèbvre (Quenast)
Abbaye de Notre Dame de St Remy (Rochefort)
Slaghmuylder (Ninove) Dendria (Aalst)
Achouffe (Houffalize)
Keersmaeker (Asse)
Silly (Silly)
Abbaye de Notre Dame de Scourmont (Chimay)
Brassico (Ghlin)
Eylenbosch (Schepdaal)
De Troch (Wambeek)
Mouterij De Neve (Schepdaal)

MAJOR BREWERIES
OF BELGIUM

✚ indicates an abbey brewery producing beer for commercial sale

Abbaye de Notre Dame de Orval (Villers-Devant-Orval)

FACING PAGE: While many of the beers in Belgium are inheritors of long traditions, the De Dolle and La Chouffe microbreweries are representative of a new generation born in the 1980s. Even their whimsical labels are refreshing. RIGHT: The Trappist ales of the Abbey of Notre Dame de Scourmont near Chimay are the best known of their unique genre.

aware that, while other countries may have had a more standardized approach to brewing practice, Belgium was a land of individualists. Each part of the country had its own brewing techniques, which resulted in beers varying greatly in strength and style, each with its own bouquet, color and palate. Each monastery also developed its own brewing methods, and these techniques have been perfected in the twentieth century to create several distinct abbey styles of beer. Today monastery brews are still based on such a tradition. Many of these beers, though not all, are dark in color. All are made with top-fermenting yeast and so are, technically speaking, ales.

The largest selling of the Trappist beers are those from the Abbey of Notre Dame of

Scourmont near Chimay, and are known by their familiar Chimay label. There are four types of Chimay Ale: the fruity Chimay Première (red on black label), the much drier Chimay CinqCents (white label), the peppery Chimay Grand Reserve (gold on black label) and the typically 'Trappist-style' Chimay blue label. Unlike most beers around the world, Trappist beers, such as those from Chimay, benefit from laying down for two to three years, and as such may be vintage dated.

The other Trappist abbeys brewing beer include Notre Dame de la Paix (also at Chimay), Notre Dame d'Orval (Orval), Westmalle (Westmalle), St Sixtus (Westvleteren), St Benedictus (Achel), Notre Dame de Brialmont (Brialmont), Notre Dame de Clairefontaine (Clairefontaine), Notre Dame de Nazareth (Brecht) and Notre Dame de Soleilmont (Soleilmont) and Notre Dame de St Remy (Rochefort). The monks at Rochefort have been brewing since 1595, but it has only been in the last quarter of the twentieth century that their unique ales have become known outside the province of Namur.

The Orval story is a particularly colorful one. In 1070, a group of Benedictine monks from Calabria, Italy, established an abbey in the Golden Valley (*val d'or*), which has come

to be transposed as Orval. During the twelfth century, at the request of Count Albert of Chiny (St Bernard of Clairvaux), the Church sent monks from Trois-Fontaines. True to Cistercian tradition, these monks from the Champagne region built their abbey along the Roman road between Rheims and Trier (Treves).

The little pond, clear and cold, next to the portal of Our Lady's Church, owes its name to the charming legend that is immortalized by the illustration on the label of Orval beer. In the eleventh century, the suzeraine of the region was Countess Matilda, duchess of Tuscany and Godfrey of Bouillon's aunt. In about 1076, she wished to see the courageous settlers from Calabria. Sitting at the edge of the spring, which was providing water to the monastery, she accidentally dropped her wedding ring into the water. This ring was a keepsake of her late husband. Overcome with its loss, the Countess ardently beseeched the Virgin Mary. Suddenly, a trout rising out of the water returned the precious ring to her. Filled with awe at what had just happened, the Countess cried out, 'Why, this is truly a "val d'or!"'

Sacked and plundered during the seventeenth century, rebuilt, enlarged and improved by its inhabitants, the abbey was then

ABOVE AND BELOW: The monks at the Abbey of Notre Dame de St Remy near Rochefort enjoy their beers at mealtime. LEFT: Notre Dame d'Orval brews a single, splendid ale. FACING PAGE: At Notre Dame de Scourmont near Chimay, brewing is under the direction of Father Theodore. The abbey's Grande Reserve (BOTTOM) is vintage dated (see cork), and is one of the only beers in the world that actually improves with aging.

bombarded in the eighteenth century by General Loison. It was in 1926 that the Abbaye d'Orval rose again from its ruins, thanks to the initiative of Dom Marie-Albert Van der Cruyssen. In 1948, after World War II, the present abbey was completed. Today some 40 monks live and work at the Abbaye d'Orval, brewing their distinctive beer.

The Abbey at Grimbergen, near Brussels, has one of the handful of abbey breweries where the monks are not Trappists. The Abbey was founded in 1128, the first of the Norbertine order. It has survived the centuries since, and today flourishes, offering strong monastery beers. Grimbergen Double is a deep red, top-fermented beer with a mild, fruity flavor and a six percent alcohol content. Grimbergen Triple, a strong, blond ale of eight percent alcohol content, is fermented three times.

Corsendonk Abbey in Oud-Turnhout was founded through the munificence of Maria van Gelre, youngest daughter of Jan III, duke of Brabant. (Jan I—Jan Primus, duke of Brabant—is today better known as Gambrinus, the patron monarch of beer.) The monks of Corsendonk started a brewery in 1400, which flourished until 1784 when the Abbey was closed by Austrian ruler Jozef II. In 1906, Antonius Keersmaekers founded a secular brewery to revive the monks' brewing traditions. His award-winning beers included Agnus Dei (Lamb of God), a light-bodied, high fermentation brew of delicate palate. Antonius' grandson Jef now continues the family tradition of brewing the Trappist-style Agnus Dei and Pater Noster (Our Father). In the United States, Agnus Dei is known as Monk's Pale Ale, and Pater Noster is known as Monk's Brown Ale.

The Abbey of Leffe, near Dinant on the banks of the River Meuse, was founded in 1152 by the Premontratesian order. In the archives, the first reference to a brewery there was in 1240 when Father Abbot bought one from Gosuin, a cleric of Dinant. Since 1954, the St Guibert Brewery at Mont St Guibert has produced the five abbey-style beers: Leffe Blonde, Radieuse, Triple, Brune and Vieille Cuvée. St Guibert also produces Vieux Temps Amber.

The St Bernardus Brewery, which is not actually an abbey brewery, is located in Watou in Flanders in the heart of the famous Popering hop-growing district. For three generations, the Claus family has brewed exclusively under the license of the tiny St Sixtus Abbey, using the Abbey recipe and brewing techniques.

RIGHT: The St Bernardus Brewery brews under license from the St Sixtus Abbey. The Tripel is a strong ale with seven percent alcohol.

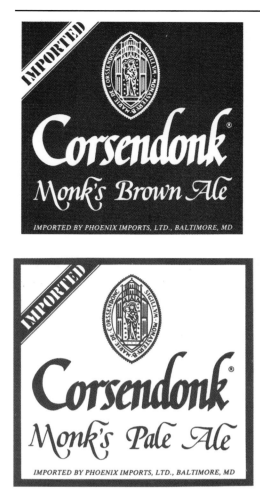

ABOVE: Export labels from the Corsendonk Abbey in Oud-Turnhout. BELOW: The Premontratesian order brews at the Abbey of Leffe near Dinant. BOTTOM: The Norbertine Abbey at Grimbergen was founded in 1128. RIGHT: Affligem is a Flemish secular 'abbey-style' beer.

LAMBIC

While the tradition of monastic brewing has survived, prospered and continued to be an important influence, it is just one of many elements in Belgium's brewing culture. Like microbreweries, farmhouse breweries have given rise to some of today's specialties and represent another fiercely independent Belgian tradition. Perhaps the most notable of these are the lambic beers from the lambic (or lembeek) region, specifically the Senne Valley, in the area south of Brussels.

Lambic beers are unique from nearly all other beers in the world in that they are produced with *neither* lager yeast nor ale yeast. They are spontaneously fermented with wild yeasts native only to that valley.

Some notable types of lambics include gueuze (a blended lambic) and unique fruit beers. The latter are brewed using fruits as a flavoring, just as other beers use hops to flavor the malt beverage. Most common fruit lambics are kriek, made with cherries, and frambozen (or framboise), made with raspberries. Other versions use various types of berries or peaches. Also included is faro, a sugary gueuze. Although fruit beers are now made in America, lambics are quite simply unlike any type of beer that can be found elsewhere in the world.

Two of the older and more important lambic brewers are Liefman's and Lindeman's. Liefman's Brewery in Oudenburg dates to 1679, but the nearby Abbey of St Arnoldus

was probably brewing beer as early as 1084. Liefman's produces both fruit ales and a brown ale (goudenband). Founded in 1811, Lindeman's farmhouse brewery in Vlezenbeek produces both gueuze and fruit lambics.

In 1887, the brewery in Itterbeek in the Senne Valley known as the 'Little Mole' was taken over by Paul Walravens, whose daughter married Franz Timmermans in 1911. Their grandsons Raoul and Jacques van Custem are the current owners of the Timmermans Brewery. As with other breweries in the Senne, Timmermans brews a wide variety of lambics, including gueuze, kriek, framboise, cassis and pêche. De Troch Brewery in Ternat-Wambeek brews the Chapeau brand of lambics that include a wider variety of fruits than a typical lambic brewer. These include such fruits as bananas, which are clearly not native to Belgium.

The Belle-Vue brewery was established in the Senne Valley in 1913 by Philemon Vanden Stock, acquiring its name in 1927 when he brought the tenancy of the Café Belle-Vue in Anderlecht. He developed the brewery, with his son Constant and son-in-law Octave Collin, until his death in 1945. After World War II, the brewery became Belgium's leading gueuze producer and today provides 75 percent of the Belgian market for that style. Belle-Vue's kriek also has a 75 percent market share. Interbrew acquired Belle-Vue in July 1991.

ABOVE: Characteristic lambic beers from a variety of brewers. Column 1 are gueuze, the blended lambic; column 2 are kriek (cherry), a popular fruit lambic; column 3 are framboise (raspberry); and column 4 are pêche (peach), a fruit lambic that has enjoyed great popularity since the 1980s. RIGHT: De Troch's portfolio also includes some unusual fruit lambics.

FACING PAGE, TOP: Belle-Vue Kriek and De Troch's Faro. Faro is a sweetish variant of gueuze lambic favored in the Brussels café scene. FACING PAGE: Cherries and raspberries bring a distinctive flavor to kriek and framboise lambics.

WITBIER

Beer, by definition, is a beverage derived from malted barley. Other grains, such as rice and cornmeal, are often used in less expensive, mass market brands as a cheaper source of starch, but this practice is frowned upon by discriminating brewers and consumers. Exceptions are made in the case of oats in English oatmeal stout and with wheat in American wheat beer, German weissbier and Flemish witbier. Both the German and Flemish terms are literally translated as meaning 'white beer.' This is a reference to the light color of the beer and the fact that it usually has yeast particles in suspension and hence it is cloudy, translucent and lighter in appearance than if it were transparent.

Flavored with coriander and curaçao as well as hops, witbier is indigenous to the wheat-producing open country in the Flemish-speaking regions of Belgium such as Flanders and Brabant. Legend holds that it originated in Hoegaarden in Brabant, but it may have been introduced from Germany. In

any case, beer has been brewed in Hoegaarden since well before the first written mention of a brewery in 1318. Begarden monks began brewing the Hoegaarden Witbier in 1445, and this wheat beer was popular throughout Belgium for five centuries, but competition from the mass market lagers caused the last brewery's closure in 1957. Hoegaardiers felt the need to revive their tradition, and in 1965 Pieter Celis again started to brew the naturally cloudy white beer. In 1992, Celis relocated to Texas where it continued the tradition with an American witbier appropriately called Celis White.

Today the De Kluis brewery in Hoegaarden keeps the tradition alive, as does Riva in Dentergems who produce an important witbier known to the export market as Dentergem's White Ale. Aromas of selected herbs sweeten the taste and character of Dentergems. The Gouden Boom (Golden Tree) Brewery in Bruges brews a witbier as do Van Eecke in Watou, Vieille Villers in Puurs and others.

FACING PAGE: The distinctive, cloudy look of Flemish witbier in the form of the Hoegaarden brand from the De Kluis brewery. RIGHT: The domestic and export labels from Hoegaarden witbier.

BELOW: The domestic and export labels for Dentergems witbier, brewed by Riva, as well as a selection of other witbiers (in French, bière blanche) from throughout Belgium. The fact that De Kluis, Riva, Van Eecke, De Gouden Boom and others use their city names as brand names for witbier indicates the high regard in which Belgians hold their 'local' witbier.

FACING PAGE, BOTTOM: The De Kluis product line includes the strong and fruity Verboden Vrucht (Forbidden Fruit) and the rich Grand Cru as well as witbier.

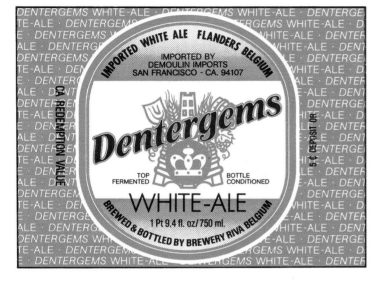

CANADA

The oldest existing brewery in the Western Hemisphere is in Canada, and brewing has been a part of the lives of Canadians since the seventeenth century. The history of brewing in Canada was similar to that of the United States—early and well-developed home brewing activity and an active brewpub scene by the eighteenth century. The first big name in commercial Canadian brewing was John Molson. From the English county of Lincolnshire, Molson arrived in Montreal in 1782 armed with a copy of John Richardson's *Theoretical Hints on the Improved Practice of Brewing.*

The people of Quebec, predominantly French, preferred wine, so there was little in the way of a brewing tradition in this province. Since imported English beer sold for more than rum in Montreal, the city's beer drinkers welcomed John Molson's first brewery, which began brewing in 1786. Today Molson Breweries (Brasseries Molson in Quebec) is the oldest brewing company in all of North America. The headquarters and the flagship brewery are located in Montreal, and the company's other breweries are located in Barrie, Ontario; Vancouver, British Columbia; Edmonton, Alberta; Winnipeg, Manitoba; Prince Albert, Saskatchewan; Regina, Saskatchewan; and St John's, Newfoundland. The Sick's Lethbridge Brewery in Lethbridge, Alberta, has been a Molson subsidiary since 1958.

Molson's flagship brand is Molson Golden, which is a national brand in Canada and the biggest selling Canadian export brew in the United States. Other Molson beers include Molson Canadian Lager, Molson Light (Legère), Molson Export Ale and Export Light Ale. Special regional beers brewed by Molson's western breweries (British Columbia, Alberta, Manitoba and Saskatchewan) are Bohemian, Brador, Edmonton Export Lager, Frontier Beer, Imperial Stout, Old Style and Royal Stout. Regional beers brewed by Molson in eastern Canada include Molson Bock, Molson Cream Porter, Molson Diamond, Molson Oktoberfest India Beer and Laurentide Ale. Molson also brews Löwenbräu under license from Löwenbräu in Munich. Since 1987 Molson has also brewed Coors in Canada, under license from the brewery in Colorado, and in 1988 Molson started contract production of Kirin Beer from Japan.

John Labatt, Ltd (Brasserie Labatt L'tee in Quebec and usually known as Labatt's) dates to a brewery built in 1828 in London, Ontario, by innkeeper George Balkwill. This brewing company was sold to William and George Snell in 1828 and to Samuel Eccles and John Labatt in 1847. In 1853, Labatt became the sole owner, and renamed the company for himself.

Labatt's flagship brand, and the leading single brand of beer, is Labatt's Pilsen, which is better known (because of its label) as 'Labatt's Blue.' As with many United States brews, Labatt's leading brand is complemented by a low-calorie beer appropriately named Blue Light. The company's other brands fall into three categories: other company-owned national brands (like 'Blue' and Blue Light); foreign brands brewed under license by Labatt in Canada; and company-

LEFT: A copper brew kettle at Moosehead's Dartmouth, Nova Scotia, brewery. FACING PAGE: Labatt's export line-up includes the famous 'Blue' and '50' Ale.

THIS PAGE: Molson's products include its flagship 'Golden' as well as Export Ale and Arctic Bay, which was introduced in 1987. Calgary was an independent Alberta brand that became part of Carling O'Keefe, which was in turn acquired by Molson in 1989. Calgary was reintroduced as an *amber* lager in 1988.

owned regional brands, which may be brewed in only one or two provinces. The national brands include Labatt 50 Ale (introduced as a special promotion in 1950), John Labatt Classic, Labatt's Light (Legère) and Labatt Select. The latter two are low-calorie beers introduced in 1978 and 1984, respectively.

Labatt's major regional brands—all derived from smaller brewers acquired over the years—are Kokanee Pilsner Beer, which is popular in British Columbia; Club Beer in Manitoba; Crystal Lager Beer in Ontario; Blue Star in Newfoundland; and Alexander Keith's India Pale Ale, which is the largest-selling brand of beer in the Maritimes. Other Labatt's regionals are Cervoise, Columbia Pilsner, Cool Spring, Country Club Stout, Extra Stock Ale, Gold Keg, Grand Prix, IPA (India Pale Ale), Jockey Club Beer, Kootenay Pale Ale, Manitoba 200, Old Scotia Ale, Schooner, Skol, Super Bock, Velvet Cream Porter, Velvet Cream Stout and White Seal Beer. A recent addition to the product list includes Twistshandy, a lemon-lime flavored beer.

In recent decades, the brewing industry in North America has introduced several project innovations in an effort to create a distinctive variation on their mass market lagers. Because the taste of North American mass market lagers is so subtle compared to other beer styles, the innovations had to be more implicit than explicit. In other words, any change that was made had to be something that didn't require taste to distinguish, but rather a barely perceptible difference that might be apparent by reading the label or through the perception that the beer was 'less filling.' The first such innovation was low calorie or 'light' beers, which were introduced in the 1970s, and 'dry' beer, which was introduced in 1990. The former was very successful, while the latter, which was similar technically, failed to generate significant market share.

In 1993, the two largest brewing companies in Canada (Molson and Labatt) and the United States (Anheuser-Busch and Miller) began to market 'ice' beer. Developed and patented by Labatt, ice beer is a pale lager which is quickly chilled to sub-freezing

temperatures after brewing but before final fermentation. The result is the formation of ice crystals in the beer, which are removed to produce a beer with roughly *twice* the alcohol content of typical mass market lagers.

Canada was, for many years, the second biggest brewing nation in North America, but yielded that distinction to Mexico in the mid-1970s. Of the big three, Labatt's is Canada's largest brewing company and Molson traditionally has had the largest Canadian share of the lucrative export market to the United States. In 1989, however, Molson and third-place Carling O'Keefe announced their intention to merge into a single entity to be called Molson Breweries. This new entity would then become Canada's premier brewer, with better than half the market.

Carling O'Keefe, Ltd (Brasserie O'Keefe L'tee in Quebec) was the result of the nineteenth century merger of the breweries of Sir John Carling (established by his father, Thomas Carling, in 1840) and of Eugene O'Keefe (established in 1862). In the 1950s and 1960s, Carling O'Keefe expanded its operations into the United States through its subsidiary company, Carling National Brewing, which once operated 14 breweries in 11 states. In fact, in 1960 Carling National was the fourth largest brewer in the United States. After this high point, the market share of the subsidiary declined, and Carling, like many other brewers, was forced into closing its American plants.

An interesting aside to the big three is that each had a flagship or most popular brand which was identified by a color. These were Carling O'Keefe's *Black* Label, Labatt's Pilsen *Blue* and Molson *Golden*.

IF IT'S NOT ICE BREWED, IT'S NOT ICE BEER.

Despite the dominance of the big three, several smaller breweries still exist and new microbreweries have been started in British Columbia and Nova Scotia since the mid-1980s. The big three were, however, the only brewing companies with breweries in more than one province, and as a result, they are the only brewers with national distribution.

Carling O'Keefe's flagship brand is Black Label Beer, which is brewed at all seven Carling O'Keefe breweries across Canada. Other brands in regional distribution include Red Cap Ale, Alta 3.9, Black Horse, Calgary Lager, Carling Pilsner, Champlain, Dominion Ale, Dow Ale, Heidelberg, Kronenbräu 1308, O'Keefe Ale, O'Keefe Extra Old Stock Malt Liquor, O'Keefe Light, Old Vienna, Standard Lager, Trilight and Toby. In addition to its own brands, Carling O'Keefe brews Miller High Life under license from Miller Brewing in the United States and Carlsberg under license from the Carlsberg Breweries of Copenhagen, Denmark.

The story of Moosehead Breweries, Canada's oldest independent brewing company, is a story of survival, perseverance and of a family rallying together to beat the odds. It all began in John and Susannah Oland's backyard in Dartmouth, Nova Scotia, in 1867. Using family recipes brought from England, they began brewing ale. Its flavor proved popular, so the Olands produced larger quantities of their 'good salable ale' to supply

the army and navy. With an investment of $7000, the 'Army & Navy Brewery' was formed on the Dartmouth, Nova Scotia, waterfront facing Hailfax. Tragedy struck three years later, when John Oland was killed after falling from his horse, and Susannah was forced to sell a controlling interest in the brewery. In 1877, an inheritance left by an English relative enabled Susannah to buy back control of the brewery, which she renamed S Oland Sons & Co.

Susannah Oland died in 1886, and her youngest son, George WC Oland, took over operation of the brewery. Because of economic hardships resulting from Prohibition, the majority of Canada's Maritime breweries were forced to sell to an English syndicate in 1895, but unlike the others, the Olands later regained control of their brewery.

In 1917, an explosion caused by the collision of two ships in Halifax Harbor destroyed the brewery, and Susannah's son and brewmaster, Conrad Oland, was killed and his brother John injured. The following year, George Oland and his eldest son,

George Bauld Oland, moved to Saint John, New Brunswick. With insurance money from the explosion, they purchased the Simeon Jones Brewery and later renamed it the Red Ball Brewery.

Although Prohibition was still in effect and the Olands were permitted to brew only two percent alcohol beer, they made enough through the New Brunswick operation to return to Halifax and build a new brewery. In 1928, George Oland took over Ready's Breweries in Saint John and called his new company New Brunswick Breweries, Ltd.

A company milestone occurred in 1931, when George Oland rechristened his ale 'Moosehead.' In 1947, the company name was changed from New Brunswick Breweries, Ltd to Moosehead Breweries, Ltd, and the Ready's Pale Ale was rechristened as 'Moosehead Pale Ale' to mark the company's entry into the Nova Scotia market.

In 1971, the Halifax branch of the Oland family, which ran a competitive operation called Keith's Brewery, decided to sell to Labatt. This left Moosehead Breweries with

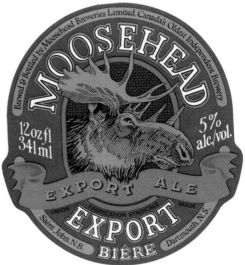

THIS PAGE: Moosehead, now Canada's third largest, dates from 1867, but did not go national until the 1990s!

FACING PAGE: Carling O'Keefe was Canada's third largest brewer when it merged with Molson in 1989. Shown here are its flagship national brand, two regionals, and the sun setting upon the brewery in York, Ontario.

MAJOR BREWERIES OF CANADA

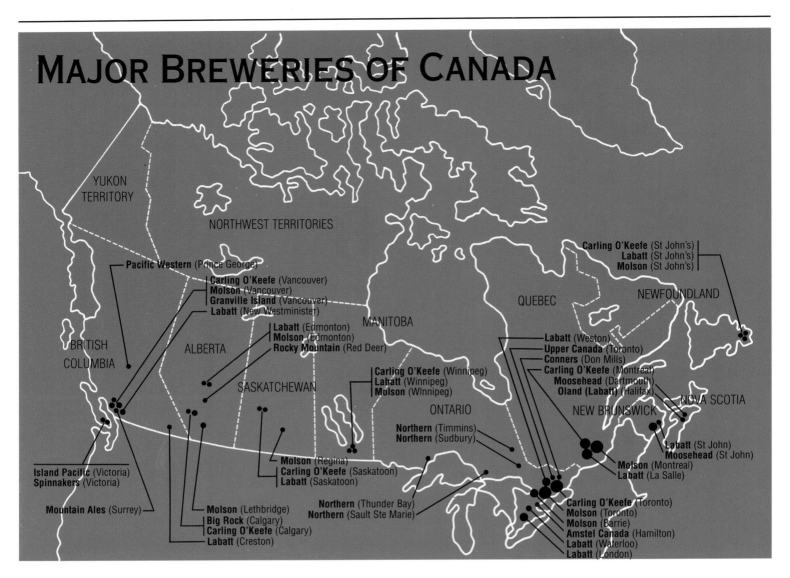

plants in Saint John, New Brunswick, and Dartmouth, Nova Scotia, making it the last major Canadian independent brewery.

It was in 1978 that Moosehead entered the United States market with their Moosehead Canadian Lager beer in bottles, and in 1984 Moosehead draft beer was introduced. By the 1990s, Moosehead was available in all 50 states and was ranked as the seventh largest import beer out of 450 brands. In 1985, Moosehead arrived in England, distributed by Whitbread. Ironically, it was not until May 1992 that Moosehead Breweries introduced its beer in the Canadian provinces of Ontario, British Columbia, Alberta and Newfoundland. In 1993, Moosehead was launched in Manitoba.

Oland Breweries, Ltd of Halifax, Nova Scotia, was founded by the same Oland family that started Moosehead, but the Oland Breweries were sold—as noted above—to Labatt in 1971. Two Oland breweries operate; the one at Halifax is called Oland Brewery and the one at Saint John, New Brunswick, is called Labatt's New Brunswick Brewery. Both breweries produce Labatt's 'Blue,' Labatt's 50 Ale and Labatt's Schooner Beer, while Halifax brews Keith's India Pale Ale and Saint John brews Labatt's Light. Both

breweries also brew Oland Export, and Halifax also produces two other Oland name brands, Oland Light and Oland Stout.

Northern Breweries, Ltd has more breweries in Canada's largest province than any other brewing company, although it is among Ontario's smaller breweries. Northern Brewing is headquartered in Sault Sainte Marie, and has breweries in suburban Thunder Bay and Timmins, which brew beer only for the draft (draught) market. Thunder Bay brews only Superior Lager and Thunder Bay, and Timmins brews only Northern Ale. The plant in Sudbury brews and bottles Northern and Encore Beer, while the Sault Sainte Marie plant brews and bottles Superior Lager, Northern Extra Light, Edelbräu, Encore, 55 Lager, Kakabeka Cream and Silver Spray.

Amstel Brewery Canada, formerly Hamilton Breweries, began operations in 1981 and is now owned entirely by Heineken NV of the Netherlands. Headquartered in Hamilton, Ontario, the products brewed here include Steeler Lager, which is considered Hamilton's 'hometown' beer, and Grizzly, a lager originally brewed only for the United States export market but now available in Ontario as well. A major part of Amstel's

operation, of course, is devoted to brewing the parent company's Amstel and Amstel Light brands. Rocky Mountain Brewing of Red Deer, Alberta, (formerly owned by 'Uncle' Ben Ginter and now a subsidiary of Steeplejack Services in Calgary) operates the only independent brewery in the fast-growing, oil-rich province on the eastern side of the Canadian Rockies.

Pacific Western Brewing of Prince George, British Columbia, was originally established on a freshwater spring in 1957 under the name Caribou Brewing. Five years later, it was bought by Carling O'Keefe and promptly auctioned off. It was purchased by Ben Ginter and rechristened Tartan Breweries. It was sold again in 1981 to WR Sharpe (formerly of Canada Dry) and his associates, who operated it as the Old Fort Brewing Company until 1984, when the name was changed to Pacific Western Brewing. In 1989, Pacific Western purchased Simcoe Brewing in Ontario and Granville Island Brewing in Vancouver. Granville Island Brewing was among the largest of the smaller breweries that opened in British Columbia in the early 1980s.

Mountain Ales of Surrey, British Columbia, was one of the several small breweries

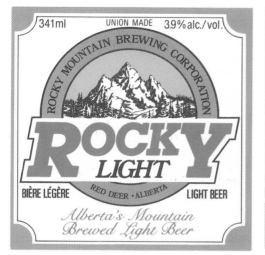

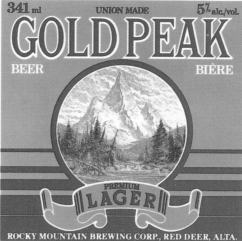

CLOCKWISE FROM ABOVE: The interests of the Oland family in Dartmouth, Nova Scotia, evolved into Moosehead, while the Halifax Olands retained the family name, but sold to Labatt in 1971. Alexander Keith's brewery was acquired by the Halifax Olands in the 1940s.

Rocky Mountain Brewing of Alberta and Northern of Ontario are two of Canada's oldest surviving independent regionals. Iron Horse was brewed by Old Fort Brewing, which became Pacific Western in 1989.

These pages illustrate the exciting world of micro-breweries that have come on the scene in Canada in the 1980s and 1990s.

Shown on this page (CLOCKWISE FROM THE LEFT) are the bottle-capping line at the Upper Canada Brewing facility in Toronto; the impressive home of the Brick Brewery in Waterloo, Ontario; Extra Ale from Ed McNally's Big Rock Brewery in Calgary, Alberta; Peculiar from the Granite Brewery in Halifax, Nova Scotia; and one of the Conners' brands, brewed at Don Mills, Ontario, since 1985.

that started in the Vancouver area in the early 1980s. Big Rock Brewery was founded in 1985 by Ed McNally and is located in Calgary, Alberta. Conners Brewing began brewing in 1985 in Don Mills, near Toronto, Ontario.

Granite Brewery of Halifax, Nova Scotia, was established in 1985 and was the first Canadian microbrewery and brewpub outside British Columbia. Upper Canada Brewing was founded by Frank Heaps in Toronto, Ontario, in 1985. The principal brands brewed there are Dark Ale, Rebellion Malt Liquor, True Bock and True Light. Strathcona Brewing of Edmonton, Alberta, is a microbrewery that was founded in 1986.

Along with the advent of microbreweries in the 1980s, brewpubs began to appear in Canada shortly after they appeared in the United States. Spinnakers Brewpub was founded in Victoria, British Columbia in May 1984, and is owned by the Spinnakers Brewing Corporation of Victoria, which also owns the two Noggins brewpubs in Seattle, Washington.

With the development of distinctive microbrewed beers in both the United States and Canada, a major issue in the 1990s on both sides of the 'world's longest undefended border' has been the availability of these beers across that border. The Canadian market has long been protected from imports—not just from Europe and the United States but also from beer from other provinces within Canada. Under the provisions of the North American Free Trade Agreement (NAFTA), the Canadian government decided to open its beer market to Americans by 1995 and to scrap the archaic restrictions on the flow of beer within Canada. The Canadian brewers complained and the United States negotiators fired back with a demand that the Canadian beer market be opened immediately.

In April 1992, Michael Wilson, Canada's trade minister, announced that the Canadian market would start treating American beer the same as Canadian beer, and Ontario, Canada's largest province where nearly half of the American imports are consumed, responded with a total ban on any and all American beer imports. This broadside hit the Americans square between the eyes, and the United States promptly threatened to slap the Canadian brewers with stinging duties on Canadian beer exported to the States. Fortunately for consumers, the issue was resolved and Canadian microbrews have begun to seep across the border, where heavy duties would have obviously hurt their makers far worse than they would Canada's giant brewers.

THIS PAGE: The Upper Canada Brewery was established in Toronto in 1985 by Frank Heaps.

EASTERN EUROPE

THE CZECH REPUBLIC

The industrialization of eastern Europe generally lagged behind that of the West and that factor affected—for both good and ill—the development of brewing. Although indigenous beer styles of the nineteenth century and before survived well into the twentieth century, World War II and the decades of Soviet domination greatly diluted the region's brewing heritage while at the same time stifling innovation.

On the other hand, one of Europe's most important brewing centers was part of the Soviet Empire until 1989. That part of

Czechoslovakia which is now the Czech Republic has a highly evolved brewing culture that dates to the Middle Ages and continues to rank with Britain, Belgium and Germany as one of the four most important brewing nations in Europe. Most of the important brewing centers in the nation are in the major cities of the region of Bohemia. The country's largest brewery is located in the capital city of Prague. This is Staropramen, which was founded in 1869. Also in Prague is a tiny brewery, or *pivovary*, called U Fleku, which dates from 1499 and is the

world's oldest brewpub. The distinctive beer brewed there has made U Fleku a mecca for beer connoisseurs worldwide, who make pilgrimages there to enjoy beer in U Fleku's labyrinthine beer hall and pleasant beer garden.

The city of Pilsen has the distinction of being one of the three corners of the Golden Triangle (the others being Munich and Vienna), where large-scale lager brewing sprang up in the early nineteenth century. The city even gives its name to the lightest, palest of the styles of lager, which are known around the world as pilsner, pilsener or simply pils. While there are many pilsners, there is only one *original* Pilsner. This is the beer, first brewed in 1842, that is known in Czech as Plzensky Prazdroj, but known around the world by the words on the distinctive white and gold label: Pilsner Urquell. The explicit Pilsner Urquell was registered in 1898 in a document that referred to 'the absurdity and illogic of using the word "Pilsner" for beer brewed in towns outside of Pilsen.' However, today the term has become generic. Pilsner Urquell was first developed by Martin Kopecky, who supported the idea of producing an outstanding beer that could replace many non-resident beers in Pilsen pubs. Production started on 5 October 1832, and the first barrels were shipped to Pilsen restaurants, but several were sent to Karel Knobloch's pub on Liliova Street in Prague, which was the first commercial draft account for the new beer. Pilsner Urquell was also a success in Bohemian spa towns such as Karlsbad, and this led to its being distributed worldwide.

FACING PAGE: At 500 years, U Fleku in Prague is the world's oldest brewpub. ABOVE: The Aldaris Brewery in Riga, Latvia, circa 1906. RIGHT: Pilsen's Prazdroj (Pilsner Urquell) is the best known Czech beer, Staropramen is the biggest Czech brewery.

By 1856, the beer from Pilsen was being served in Vienna, and three years later it had reached Paris. Beginning on 1 October 1900, the Pilsen 'beer train' left early every morning for Vienna. A similar train also went to Bremen. By 1874, this Czech beer had arrived in America. The path to the world had begun. As Pilsner Urquell became established in European cities, from Lvov to London, it began to receive medals and honors from international shows and exhibitions.

The brewery at Pilsen reached an annual production of over 800,000 barrels (one million hectoliters) before World War I, but that number would not be exceeded for many decades because of the world wars. Also, the years between 1919 and 1923, in the aftermath of the First World War, were quite difficult for Czech industry. The domestic market was reduced and many markets abroad were lost. Brewery production gradually declined because of decreasing market-

ing possibilities, and an increasing lack of raw materials and manpower.

In the late 1930s, production rebounded, and the Pilsner breweries accounted for 75 to 85 percent of the the entire beer export from the country. Production levels fell again during World War II. The Communist government seized the brewery after the war, and by 1956 Pilsner Urquell was once again being exported, bringing in much-needed hard currency for the brewery's new masters. Successive plant modernizations between 1965 and 1985 prepared the original Pilsner for the inevitable market expansion that followed the collapse of Communism in 1989. This event also opened the door to the poten-

tial of a wider range of Czech beers reaching Western markets. While Pilsen is legendary, another important brewing center is the Czech city of Ceske Budejovice, which was known in German as Budweis during the days of the Austro-Hungarian Empire in the late nineteenth century. The beer of the city's major brewery was—and still is—known as Budweiser. As the story goes, Adolphus Busch of Anheuser-Busch selected the beers of this region as the model for the national brand he introduced in the United States in 1876. Today both Budweisers still exist, but not in the same markets, and there is no similarity in taste. The Czech Budweiser is actually known as Budvar at home.

ELSEWHERE IN EASTERN EUROPE

There are also indigenous brewing industries in Hungary, Bulgaria, Poland, Slovenia, Croatia, Serbia and the constituent republics of the former Yugoslavia. Their products had begun appearing in the West even before the collapse of Communism, and in October 1991, the Belgian-based Interbrew Group acquired the Borsodi Sorgyar brewery in Bocs, Hungary. Especially visible in the West are the beers of the Warsaw Brewery. The firm's main plant and headquarters are situated in the center of Poland's capital city on Grzybowska Street. The company was established in 1848 and has operated continuously at the same loca-

tion with a malt mill, bottling line and three retail shops in Warsaw and breweries in Kutno, Wyszkow and Ciechanow.

The former Soviet Union was one of the world's largest brewing nations, ranking fifth behind the United States, Germany, Britain and Japan. Russia still is a major producer, but the transition to a market economy has necessitated some fundamental changes, as has been the case in all industries there. For nationally-controlled factories, the breweries of the old USSR had a surprising level of brand identification. While most Soviet breweries had such inspired names as State Brewery (PBZ) No 136, others—notably in

Lithuania, Latvia and Estonia, as well as Russia—dated to the days before the 1917 Revolution. One of the important brewers in the Baltic region is the Aldaris Brewery in Riga, Latvia, which dates from 1865. Aldaris produces porter (porteris), that has been important in the Baltic region since the big English brewers started exporting porter to the region in the nineteenth century.

As the beer markets of Eastern Europe become more integrated with those of Western Europe and the rest of the world, many delightful, but under-recognized brands are taking their rightful place with beer lovers everywhere.

ABOVE AND BELOW (TOP): Aldaris, a major brewery in Riga, Latvia, dates from 1865. BOTTOM: Krolewskie is one of the best-recognized brands in the cafés of Warsaw, Poland.

FACING PAGE, ABOVE: Budvar (Budweiser) is brewed in the Czech city of Ceske Budejovice (Budweis). FACING PAGE, BELOW: This Czech beer hall bears the logo of the original Pilsen-style lager, first brewed in Pilsen in 1842.

MAJOR BREWERIES OF EASTERN EUROPE

Badajev Pivoarennij Zavod (Moscow, Russia)

Aldaris (Riga, Latvia)

Pivovarennij Zavod Starovilenkaja (Minsk, Belorus)

Plzensky Prazdroj (Pilsner Urquell) (Pilsen, Czech Republic)

Zaklady (Poznan, Poland)

Zaklady (Warsaw) (Warsaw, Poland)

Prazské (Prague, Czech Republic)

Staropramen (Prague, Czech Republic)

Pivovarennij Zavod, Ul. Pivoarennaja (Kiev, Ukraine)

U Fleku (Prague, Czech Republic)

Zaklady (Glubczyce, Poland)

Zaklady (Żywiec, Poland)

Zaklady (Tychy, Poland)

Zaklady (Brzesko-Okocim, Poland)

Budvar (Ceské Budejovice)

Stredoslovenské (Martin, Slovakia)

Vychodoslovenské (Kosice, Slovakia)

Séveromoravské (Prerov, Czech Republic)

Zapadoslovenské (Bratislava, Slovakia)

Jihomoravské (Brno, Czech Republic)

Union (Ljublijana, Slovenia)

Köbányai (Budapest, Hungary)

Borsodi (Böcs, Hungary)

Nagykanizsai (Nagykanizsa, Hungary)

Karlovacka (Karlovac, Croatia)

Zagrebacka (Zagreb, Croatia)

BIP (Belgrade, Serbia)

Bosanska Krajina (Banja Luka, Bosnia-Herzegovina)

Bulgarsko (Sofia, Bulgaria)
Bulgarsko (Sofia, Bulgaria)
Kombinat Sofijisko (Sofia, Bulgaria)
Lulim (Sofia, Bulgaria)
Vitosha (Sofia, Bulgaria)

SOUTHERN EUROPE

Historically, the lands surrounding the Mediterranean were a region of vineyards, a land where wine and wine-making flourished and became an art form. We are even told by certain beer-denigrating beverage historians that the people of northern Europe drank beer only because they couldn't grow grapes for wine!

That beverage squeezed from the grape is still an important part of the diet—as well as the industry—of the Mediterranean. Italy, which the ancient Greeks called *Oenotria* (the land of wine) produces more wine than France. Spain, Portugal and Greece are also major producers and consumers of wine,

with Spain having more acres of vineyards than either France or Italy. In fact, in Portugal 15 percent of the population is involved in the wine industry. However, beer is actually taking *away* market share—albeit a tiny sliver—from wine, especially in the cities of Spain and Italy where beer drinking is developing a cachet among younger drinkers that reminds one of the brasserie scene in Paris. In Italy, for example, per capita consumption of beer increased from 14 to 24 liters between 1975 and 1985.

Predictably, a large share of the beer market in southern Europe is dominated by northern European imports. Heineken of the

Netherlands owns breweries in Italy, Spain and Greece. Not to be discounted, though, are several important local brewing companies. The largest brewer in southern Europe is Peroni in Rome, followed by Heineken-owned El Aguila in Madrid, Heineken-owned Dreher in Milan and SA Damm in Barcelona, with Uniao Cervejaria in Portugal close behind. Another prominent smaller brewery—especially in the export market—is Moretti in Udine, Italy, near the Austrian border. While most southern European beers are pale pilsners, Moretti and Peroni are noted for their La Rossa, a distinctive dark red beer, and Red Ribbon, both of which are reminiscent of Munich-style lagers.

Birra Peroni Industriale was founded in Vigevano in 1846 by Francesco Peroni and relocated to Rome in 1867 by Giovanni Peroni. In 1907, the company acquired the ice-making plant near Porta Pia and formed the 'Societa Birra Peroni—Ice and Cold Storage.' In 1924, Peroni built a new plant in Bari, and in 1929 took over Birrerie Meridionali Southern Breweries in Naples. The growth of Peroni continued with its takeovers of the Dormisch Brewery in the northern Italian town of Udine, the Itala Pilsen Brewery of Padova, and the Raffo Brewery in Taranto, as well as the Faramia Brewery in Savigliano.

In the 1960s, Peroni opened three new, state-of-the-art breweries in Bari, Rome and Padova, and in 1988, the company acquired Wuhrer. The brewing of Peroni takes place throughout Italy, from San Cipriano Po, near

LEFT: Big, burnished aluminum mash tuns at Peroni's brewery in Rome. FACING PAGE: This enigmatic beer-drinker has graced Moretti's labels since 1942.

Pavia, to Bari in the south, from Rome to Naples, from Padova to Battipaglia.

The second most familiar Italian brand was founded by Luigi Moretti in Udine in 1859. The Moretti label's famous painting of the man with the mustache is based on a photograph taken in a café in 1942 by Manazzi Moretti. The image is now familiar throughout Italy, Europe and much of the world. In 1989, a large stake in Moretti was acquired by Labatt, Canada's second largest brewer. Labatt also acquired Prinz Bräu in Crespellano, Italy.

Another important player in the Italian market had been the Cisalpina Group, which was mostly owned by the Luciano family until the 1960s. The group included Pedavena in Pedavena, Dreher in Trieste, Cervisia in Genoa, Metzger in Turin and Bosio & Caratsch also in Turin. Each of these breweries was autonomous and sold beer under its own brand name. The Netherlands' Heineken acquired a minority share in the group and helped it to modernize and built a new brewery in Massafra in 1963. Cisalpina took over the Macomer Brewery on Sardinia in 1964, and the various breweries were grouped under the Dreher name. Dreher was made the group's national brand, and the regional brands were gradually discontinued.

In 1974, Heineken reached an agreement with its British licensing partner Whitbread to purchase a controlling share in Dreher, but Whitbread's initial enthusiasm for Dreher disappeared because of Dreher's financial and marketing difficulties. Dreher recovered slowly in the 1970s, and by 1980 it was a wholly-owned Heineken subsidiary.

Outdated breweries in Turin and Trieste were closed, and Heineken and Dreher production was concentrated in the breweries in Pedavena, Massafra, Macomer and Genoa. In central Italy, the former Moretti Brewery in Popoli was taken over in April 1980, and in Sardinia, the Ichnusa Brewery was acquired in 1986.

By the 1990s, Dreher held 17 percent of the market (with its major brands, Heineken, Dreher and McFarland), compared to Peroni, with a market share of 24.5 percent. Surprisingly, Peroni held a license for brewing and selling Amstel beer from April 1981 until early 1989.

In Spain, indigenous brewers had an opportunity to grow without competition until the second half of the twentieth century. The Spanish market remained closed to imported beer until 1960, with the exception of small quantities of German and Danish beer sold there in the 1950s. In 1960, Spain signed a trade agreement with the Benelux nations, and a small volume of Heineken

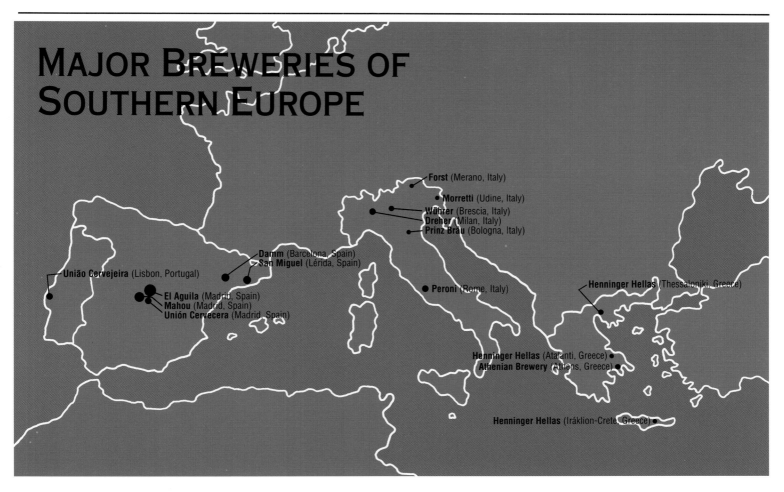

MAJOR BREWERIES OF SOUTHERN EUROPE

Forst (Merano, Italy)
Morretti (Udine, Italy)
Wührer (Brescia, Italy)
Dreher (Milan, Italy)
Prinz Bräu (Bologna, Italy)
Damm (Barcelona, Spain)
San Miguel (Lérida, Spain)
União Cervejeira (Lisbon, Portugal)
El Aguila (Madrid, Spain)
Mahou (Madrid, Spain)
Unión Cervecera (Madrid, Spain)
Peroni (Rome, Italy)
Henninger Hellas (Thessaloniki, Greece)
Henninger Hellas (Atalánti, Greece)
Athenian Brewery (Athens, Greece)
Henninger Hellas (Iráklion-Crete, Greece)

CLOCKWISE FROM BELOW: Leading brands from southern Europe include Damm of Barcelona in Spain; Dreher of Milan in Italy; Peroni of Rome and elsewhere in Italy; and Spain's El Aguila, based in Madrid.

entered the market during the next decade. During the 1970s, Spanish beer consumption increased from 32 liters per capita in 1970 to 51 in 1978. With a market share of 21 percent, El Aguila (The Eagle) led the Spanish market in the 1980s, but was losing market share and was seen as not taking adequate advantage of the expanding beer market in Spain during that period. In 1984, Heineken purchased the 84-year-old brewing company and concentrated production in four of El Aguila's seven breweries, specifically those in Madrid, Cordoba, Valencia and Zaragoza.

Spain's other big brewing company originated with Augusto R Damm, who learned his trade in the Alsace region of France and founded his Barcelona brewery in 1876. The Damm family later joined with other brewers, such as Juan Musolas (brewers of La Bohemia) and E Cammany y Cia (who later came to be known as Puigjaner y Cia). Having evolved from this merger, today's SA Damm group offers the market a wide range of products that have allowed it to establish a reputation as one of the leading brewers on the Iberian peninsula. Its breweries in Barcelona, Sta Coloma de Gramenet and El Prat de Liobregat, together with the maltery in Bell-Lloc, are well-equipped. As an aside, SA Damm also maintains an active presence in social, cultural and sporting events. For example, SA Damm was a sponsor of the 1992 Olympic Games in Barcelona.

Greece has traditionally had the lowest per capita beer consumption of any country in Europe. On a visit to Greece in the 1950s, one would have found the Fix and Alfa lagers brewed by the Fix Brewing Company in Athens and Thessaloniki, and virtually no imports. Within a decade, the big Danish and Dutch brewers, along with Beck's from Hamburg, were starting to market their products there, primarily in tourist areas. In 1965, Amstel opened a brewery—the Athenian Brewery—in Athens in partnership with local interests. At that time, Fix was owned by the former Greek defense minister, so preference or lack of preference for the government was represented in beer sales. When he resigned his government post, Amstel's market share increased.

The German brewing company Henninger opened a brewery on the island of Crete in 1971, and Heineken opened a brewery in Thessaloniki in 1975. By acquiring Amstel, Heineken also had an interest in the Athenian Brewery. Meanwhile, Spaten of Munich entered into a license brewing arrangement with Fix, and the new Brewery of Greece in Patras began to brew Löwenbräu. By 1981, Carlsberg had a brewing plant at Atalanti. The remarkably good beer market in Greece collapsed in the mid-1980s due to increased taxes under the Socialist regime. Brewery of Greece, Carlsberg and Fix were all victims, but Athenian flourished and eventually acquired the Löwenbräu rights.

WESTERN EUROPE
AND
SCANDINAVIA

AUSTRIA

With the exception of Belgium, which exists as a world apart, the brewing traditions of Western Europe and Scandinavia have largely been influenced by Germany. Even in the Netherlands, where a Belgian influence still thrives, the leading brand, Heineken, was originally inspired by German lager.

As in other German-speaking kingdoms of Europe, brewing began in what is now Austria well over a thousand years ago, and was well established by the seventeenth century. The definitive beer of the region, the Vienna style of lager, was first brewed by Anton Dreher at Schwechat near Vienna in the 1840s. Today, as with Germany, but distinctly unlike France, the Netherlands and Denmark, Austria has no dominant national brand, but rather several well-established regional brands. These brewers are in turn part of larger marketing groups. The biggest is the Osterreichische Bräu Aktiengesellschaft (Austrian Brew Corporation) or BräuAG, with headquarters at Linz in northern Austria between Vienna and Salzburg.

Founded in 1475 and 1710, respectively, Hofbräu Kaltenhausen near Salzburg and Wieselburger in Wieselburg are part of the BräuAG Group, Austria's largest brewing organization. The products are generally pale lagers, with the exception of Doppel Malz, which is a dark double bock, and Edelweiss, which is a weiss (wheat) beer.

The second largest is the Steirische Bräuindustrie Aktiengesellschaft (Styrian Brew Industry Corporation), which is headquartered at Graz in the province of Steirmark (Styria) in southern Austria. The Steirische Group includes Puntigamer and Reininghaus of Graz, as well as the well-known Gösser Bräuerei at Göss. Gösser dates to 1459, when it was founded as a monastic brewery. The brewery was acquired by Max Kober in 1860, and from that time it evolved as one of Austria's most widely distributed brands.

There are also many smaller local brewers in Vienna and throughout Austria. There is the Adambräuerei, whose logo is the conical dome of Windegg Castle at Wieten, near Innsbruck, which Josef Adam transformed into a brewery in 1825. Since the incorporation of Wilten parish into Innsbruck in 1905, the brewery has been based in Innsbruck. However, the old Wilten coat of arms has been retained in the firm's emblem. In 1917, a group of 38 Innsbruck innkeepers formed a cooperative and bought the Adambräu in

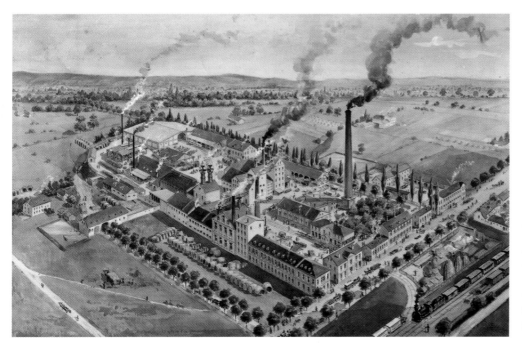

LEFT: The Puntigamer brewing facilities at Graz, Austria, as they appeared circa 1890. RIGHT: Gösser Gold is a new addition to a line that dates to 1459.

ABOVE: Today, Ottakringer is the definitive Viennese brewery. LEFT: 'Carinthian Opener' reads this poster for Villacher, brewed in the Austrian state of Carinthia since 1858. BELOW: Kaiser and Wieselburger are part of the portfolio of brands of the BräuAG Group, Austria's largest brewing organization.

order to supply their own restaurants and inns with sufficient beer of first-rate quality. In 1979 and 1981, on the occasion of the World Beer Exhibitions in Brussels and Amsterdam, Adambräu was awarded Gold Medals for its Gletscher Pils and Diat Pils.

The Johann Kuehtreiber Brewery was founded in the city of Laa on the Thaya in 1454. Kuehtreiber brews Hubertus Bräu, whose labels feature the distinctive stag of Saint Hubert. The saint is identified with Ladislaus Postumus, duke of Austria, king of Bohemia and king of Hungary, who was also a brewer of some note and whose festival brews are seen as the ancestors of current Kuehtreiber products. Vereinigte Karntner BräuereinAG was founded in 1858 in Villach, which is midway between Innsbruck and Graz.

In Vienna itself, the leading brewery is Ottakringer Bräuerei HarmerAG, which was founded in 1837 just as the lager revolution was about to change the course of brewing history. Lagers have played an important role in Ottakringer's product line, which also has included Christmas and other seasonal beers. Today the brewery's beers are marketed under the Gold Fassl brand.

TOP: Kuehtreiber in Laa brews the beer named for St Hubertus. RIGHT AND BELOW: Adambräu, both the rich Märzen and the pale UrHell, is brewed in Innsbruck, in a brewery with good rail transportation.

THESE PAGES: The Steirische Bräuindustrie Aktiengesellschaft (Styrian Brew Industry Corporation) is a holding company for three major brewing companies in Steirmark (Styria). Reiningshaus and Puntigamer are based in Graz, while Gösser hails from the town of Göss, where it was established in 1840.

Puntigamer is promoted with a hot air balloon (TOP LEFT), while the people from Gösser are always willing to tap a keg (FACING PAGE TOP) to enliven a party.

DENMARK

While lager beer was invented in central Europe, it was in Denmark that the first pure single strain of lager yeast—*Saccharomyces carlsbergensis*—was developed. As the name suggests, it was named for Scandinavia's largest brewing company—Carlsberg of Copenhagen. As the story goes, Emil Christian Hansen brought lager yeast from Germany in 1875 in a top hat, which he preserved by continuously refilling it with cold water. Once back in Copenhagen, he carefully bred the *pure* lager yeast which is now officially known by the Latin appellation *Saccharomyces carlsbergensis*.

Carlsberg as a brewing company was founded by JC Jacobsen, who was born in 1811, the son of an already-established Danish brewer, Christen Jacobsen of Copenhagen. At that time, Denmark was far from

being an important brewing center like Britain and Germany. The elder Jacobsen, aware of Denmark's reputation, tried to teach his son a more scientific and systematic approach to the brewer's art by enrolling him at the newly established Copenhagen Technical University.

In 1835, Christen Jacobsen died, leaving his 24-year-old son sole heir to one of Denmark's most advanced breweries. By this time, lager beer had suddenly captured the imagination of the world's beer drinkers, so Jacobsen made several trips to Germany in order to learn more about the lager brewing revolution. It was here that he became acquainted with bottom-fermented lager. In 1845, Jacobsen acquired a piece of land in the Copenhagen suburb of Valby and built his first brewery—the Carlsberg Brewery—named for his son Carl.

ABOVE: The famous gate at Carlsberg's Copenhagen brewery is the company's emblem. Elephant is a strong lager. BELOW: The flagship lager in export packaging. FACING PAGE: Carlsberg produces 78,000 bottles hourly.

Production of the first Carlsberg beer began on 10 November 1847, and this date is still celebrated today as Carlsberg's anniversary. Jacobsen later established a second brewery for Carl. Inaugurated in 1881, it was known as 'Ny Carlsberg' (New Carlsberg), as opposed to JC Jacobsen's own breweries which were called 'Gamie Carlsberg' (Old Carlsberg). JC Jacobsen died in 1887, and in 1906 Gamie Carlsberg and Ny Carlsberg were merged into a single entity, the Carlsberg Breweries.

Carlsberg products include Kongens Bryg, celebrating a 1454 royal brewhouse (bryghus) and featuring gold medals for barley and hops. Danske LA is Carlsberg's low-alcohol lager brand, and was one of the first beers of this kind to be available nationally on draft. The label features Holger Danske,

the guardian of the Danes, who allegedly resides in the vaults of Kronborg Castle in Elsinore—home of Carlsberg's Wiibroe subsidiary brewery—where he is fastened to his table by his beard. In the event of a national catastrophe, it is said that Holger will sever his beard and rise to the aid of the Danish people.

For many years Denmark's second biggest brewing company was Tuborg, which was founded in 1873. Relations between Tuborg and Carlsberg had always been generally good, and in 1970, as Denmark entered the European Common Market, the two merged into an entity known as the Carlsberg Group. Like the Netherlands' Amstel, when it joined the Heineken Group in 1968, Tuborg retained its own brand identity and continues to be brewed at its own plant in

Copenhagen. Since the Carlsberg/Tuborg merger, Denmark's second largest brewer has been Ceres, of which Carlsberg is now a part owner.

Ceres products include Christmas (Jule) beer and a Dortmund-style lager. Ceres' Paaske Hvidtol is a wheat beer brewed for Easter. Ceres is based in Arhus, and is allied with Thor Brewing as part of the Jutland Group, which has breweries in Hjorring, Randers and Horsens.

Founded in 1859, Albani is one of Denmark's oldest brewers. Giraf is a popular brand brewed at Odense by Albani. The Faxe Bryggeri (brewery), located in Fakse south of Copenhagen, produces a light wheat beer (Lys Faxe Hvidtol), an Easter brew (Paskebryg) and an export to Germany called 'The Great Dane' (Der Grosse Dane).

FACING PAGE: Tuborg, for many years Denmark's second biggest brewer, won an appointment to the Royal Danish Court. Long the friendly rival of the giant Carlsberg, Tuborg became part of the Carlsberg Group when Denmark joined the common market in 1970.

RIGHT: Independent brewer Albani in Odense is noted for its Giraf strong lager (which is known as a 'malt liquor' in the American market).

BELOW: Not all Scandinavian beers are lagers. Ceres brews the traditional Danish Hvidtol, a festival beer for Christmas and springtime. 'Hvidtol' literally translates as 'white beer', although it is actually dark red.

ABOVE: Although now merged with Carlsberg, Tuborg still maintains a strong brand identity. Completed in 1965, the Tuborg office building is a Copenhagen landmark. LEFT: Inside the Tuborg brewhouse, new stainless steel brewing vessels exist amid architectural details that date from 1873 when the building was built. BELOW: Carlsberg's Dansk Low Alcohol Lager was a new product introduced in the 1990s.

FINLAND

The largest brewer in Finland is Sinebrychoff (aka Koff), with plants in Helsinki, Tampere and Pori. Founded by Nikolai Sinebrychoff in 1819, 'Koff' produces a variety of lagers, including Nikolai, Light Beer and of course, Koff. Brewing takes place at Pori and at a new plant in Kerava. The old plant at Hietalahti near Helsinki ended production in 1993. Olvi Oy, one of Finland's oldest existing brewers, was established in 1878 and is now headquartered in Iisalmi, Finland.

In Finnish packaging nomenclature, Roman numerals represent the relative percentage of alcohol, ranging from I (2.8 percent) to IVA (5.2 percent). For example, Olvi Special III is the top seller, followed by Olvi Silver III. Herttun Erikoisolut IVA is a seasonal beer. Samdels III is the oldest Olvi product.

Oy Hartwall was founded in 1884, and although its headquarters and bottling plant are in Helsinki, brewing takes place at other sites in Finland, such as Lappeenranta and Torino. Lapin Kulta, Hartwall's flagship export brand, is brewed at Torino, which is in Lapland, near the Swedish border.

Oy Mallasjuoma was founded on 31 January 1912 by Finnish manufacturer Henrik Mattsson and his two sons, the brewer Ernst and the banker Max. By June 1912, production was running and marketing began with an announcement in the local newspaper, 'appetizing root beer which is sold by liters at the factory as well as in kegs transported to home.' While Prohibition was in force in Finland from 1917 to 1932, soft drinks were 'taken into Mallasjuoma's assortment.'

Today, Oy Mallasjuoma has three plants. The main brewery, which is the greatest single brewery in Finland, is in Lahti, with other factories situated in Heinola and in Oulu. The beers of Oy Mallasjuoma include Lahden and Sininen, both of which are lagers.

ABOVE TOP: Hartwall's line includes strong lagers, designated as IVA for the domestic market. ABOVE: Olvi Oy's portfolio includes Mieto and Herttun, the latter designed as celebration beer with regal airs. RIGHT: Mallasjuoma has created an appropriate beer to celebrate winter. FACING PAGE TOP: Sinebrychoff's new brewing facility at Kerava replaced their old Hietalahti brewery near Helsinki in 1993. FACING PAGE: Sinebrychoff's product line ranges from an old-fashioned Baltic Porter to a high-alcohol (IVA) lager.

FRANCE

Although in France people drink more wine than beer, they drink far more beer per capita than the English, Germans or Americans drink wine. Americans drink less than one liter of wine for every 10 liters of beer. In Britain, the ratio is slightly more than one to 10, and in Germany—a nation with its own wine industry—the ratio is one to two. The French, on the other hand, drink four liters of beer for every seven liters of wine.

French cuisine is the *haute* of *haute cuisine*, and French wine is inextricably linked with French cuisine. Against this backdrop, it would seem that beer would have little place. However, quite the opposite is true. As with French cuisine and French viticulture, French beers are brewed with care and attention to the fine subtleties of flavor. Like French wines, French beers are carefully

designed to accompany specific foods, and they succeed superbly. As Michael Jackson so aptly pointed out, the word *brasserie*, which implies a typical Parisian *café*, actually means *brewery*. What do Parisians typically drink in their brasseries? *Bière*.

Indeed, Paris has an important brewing tradition that dates back to the Roman era, when Paris was called Lutecia. In the eighteenth century, Saint Louis protected the breweries with regulations, and by the time of the French Revolution, 28 breweries existed in Paris, principally in the marshy area called La Glacière (The Glacier), where they took advantage of the special qualities of the water. During the winter, ice was harvested from the area and kept in caves for use in late summer. It was here that the master brewers of Paris prepared a brew called 'Brune de Paris' (Brown of Paris) because of

its amber color. Last in the line of Parisian breweries, and still actively brewing fine beer, the Brasserie de Lutèce was founded in 1920 on the site of the old Brasserie de la Glacière brewery.

Outside Paris, there are two principle brewing regions in France. First is the Artois region in the northeast adjacent to Belgium and centered around Lille and Armentières. It is in the latter city that Brasserie Sebastien Artois, now part of the Interbrew Group, brews Palten, Platzen, Sernia and Vezelise, as well as producing Interbrew's Belgian brands—primarily lagers—for the French market.

Two other important breweries in the northeast are Brasserie St Leonard and Brasserie Jeanne d'Arc (Joan of Arc). The latter was established in 1895 in Ronchin, a small town known for its pure well water.

CLOCKWISE FROM ABOVE: This portfolio of beers from northern France includes Belgian-influenced Platzen, Piedboeuf and Sernia from Armentières; Lutèce from Paris and Lille's extraordinary St Leonard.

RIGHT: Lutèce was founded in 1920, but is linked to a lineage going back to breweries built by the Romans.

FACING PAGE: Brasserie du Pêcheur at Schiltigheim in the Alsace, circa 1890. It now brews Fischer products.

Ronchin is located near Lille, the capital of French Flanders, which is the heir of a long brewing tradition always shared with the neighboring Belgian region of the same name. After the 1930s, the Brasserie Jeanne d'Arc developed in the region as it remained a family firm. Today, the company orients its production to classic specialty beers which are well-known in the regional market and abroad. It is the fourth largest brewery in the north of France, brewing Cristalor, Alsatia, Pilsor, Orpal and Gold Triumph lagers, as well as Scotch Triumph, a Dutch-style brown beer and two amber seasonal beers, Bière Noel for Christmas and Bière de Mars for the spring.

The most important brewing center in France is, however, the Alsace. This region, which was part of Germany from 1871 to 1918 and again from 1940 to 1944, is a place where German and French culture have been interwoven for centuries. Indeed, the cuisine of the Alsace represents the best of both cultures and is a gastronomical wonderland. The heart of the Alsace is the city of Strasbourg, which is situated on the Rhine River across from Germany. The home of the European Parliament, Strasbourg is considered to be the political centerpoint of Europe itself.

The city of Strasbourg is also the headquarters of Brasseries Kronenbourg, which is by far the largest brewery in the country and the maker of France's most important export beer. The company also, ironically, brews more beer than any brewing company in Germany. Kronenbourg was founded in Strasbourg in June 1664, within a few yards of the old customs house on the banks of the Ill River, when Jerome Hatt, a newly certified master brewer, had just married and had attached his seal to the first barrel of beer produced in his brewery, known as Brasserie

RIGHT: Brasserie Jeanne d'Arc's Orpal Lager and Scotch Triumph. Curiously, dark ale identified as 'Scotch' is a popular style in French Flanders and nearby Belgium. BELOW: Brewed in the Alsace, Kronenbourg is France's biggest brand. FACING PAGE: Posed here with hops and barley, Fischer's golden lager is also brewed in the Alsace. The distinctive cap is typical of a past era.

du Canon. By 1670, the brewery had become the favorite meeting place of the people of Strasbourg. As the years rolled by, the Hatt family passed control of the brewery from father to son, and in 1850 Guillaume Hatt decided to move his brewing activities to the heights of the suburb of Kronenbourg. By 1852, the beers of Alsace began to reach the cafés of Paris in significant quantities. In 1867, Kronenbourg was awarded several gold medals at the Universal Exhibition in Paris, which put them in the same class as competitors in Vienna and Munich. Today, Kronenbourg is Europe's largest selling bottled beer.

The second biggest brewer in the Alsace—and the third largest in France—is the Fischer Group in Schiltigheim, which dates back to 1821 and includes Brasserie du Pêcheur and Grande Brasserie Alsacienne d'Adelschoffen. Their Fischer brand is nearly as well-known in some export markets as Kronenbourg. The Adelshoffen labels stress the Strasbourg Cathedral and include a wide range of graphic styles, from the traditional to the more modern, for their Alsator low-alcohol beer.

The Brasserie du Pêcheur in Schiltigheim brews the flagship brands for the Fischer Group, which include the premium La Belle Strasbourgeoise and Kriek, a Belgian-style cherry beer. Other products include 36/15 Pêcheur and Alsa, a series of beers that celebrate the fact that the European Parliament meets in Strasbourg. Du Pêcheur also markets FischerLei and Panache non-alcoholic beers, and produces private label lagers for Bennet's and J Sainsbury in England.

At nearby Hochfelden, brewing had begun by at least 870 AD, and it was here in 1640 that Jean Klein built his first brewery, an establishment that was to remain in his family for two centuries until it was sold to the Metzger family, who became linked by marriage to the Haag family—brewers from Inguiller—in 1898. In 1927, Louis Haag created the Meteor brand, which today is the brewery's flagship label.

IMMEDIATELY ABOVE AND LEFT: Meteor and Ackerland are brewed in the Alsatian village of Hochfelden. Meteor is a lager created in 1927 by Louis Haag. ELSEWHERE ON THIS PAGE: The products of Brasserie du Pêcheur include Fischer, the cleverly packaged 36.15 and a Belgian-style kriek (Bière à la Cerise, or Cherry Beer). FACING PAGE: Today part of the Fischer Group, Adelshoffen brews in Schiltigheim, just outside Strasbourg.

LUXEMBOURG

Located between Belgium, France and
Germany in the Ardennes highlands
at the headwaters of the Moselle River, Luxembourg is literally the heart of Western
Europe. It is also bordered by three of the
most important brewing countries in Western Europe, each of which represents a distinctive brewing tradition. In Luxembourg,
however, the taste in beer runs generally to
pils. The three largest brewing companies
are Diekirch, Mousel and Brasserie
Nationale.

Mousel is an amalgam of Brasserie
Altmünster, founded in 1511, and Brasserie
Mansfeld, founded in 1563. The present flag-
ship brand at Mousel is Pils, but the product
line also includes Altmünster and Henri
Funck lagers, as well as Donkle (dark) and
Clausen, a lager marketed as a 'low alcohol'
beer that actually has less alcohol than North
American non-alcoholic beers.

Brasserie Nationale was formed in 1975 as
a merger of Brasserie Funck-Bricher and
Brasserie Bofferding, which were founded in
1764 and 1842, respectively. It was decided
at the time of the merger to focus the new
company's entire brewing effort on a single
brand, Bofferding, which is brewed in a facility located in the city of the same name.

NORWAY
AND SWEDEN

The ancient Norse, like the Celts,
drank beverages made with fermented grains because the climate of the
regions north of the 54th parallel were
hardly conducive to the growing of grapes
for wine. This development influenced the
Anglo-Saxons, who in turn influenced and
were influenced by the Celts. Indeed, the
English word *ale* probably originated with
the Norse word *aul* or the Danish *oel* (as did
the modern Danish and Norwegian *ol*).

The Norsemen and their fermented beverages notwithstanding, Norway's first modern
commercial brewery was not founded until
1776. Today, the largest brewing companies
in central Scandinavia are Pripps at both
Gothenberg and Bromma in Sweden, and
Ringnes (part of the Noral Group) in Oslo,
Norway.

MAJOR BREWERIES OF WESTERN EUROPE AND SCANDINAVIA

FINLAND
NORWAY
SWEDEN

Östersunds Bryggeri (Östersund)
Dahls (Trondheim)
Hansa (Bergen)

Oy Olvi (Iisalmi)

Pripps (Sundsvall)
Oy Mallasjuoma (Lahti)
Oy Sinebrychoff (Helsinki)
Oy Hartwall (Helsinki)

Ringnes (Oslo)
Aass (Drammen)
Arendals Bryggeri (Arendal)
Pripps (Bromma)

Pripps (Goteborg)
Abro (Vimmerby)
DENMARK
Falken (Falkenburg)
Thor (Randers)
Ceres (Arhus)
Pripps (Malmo)
Albani (Odense)
Wiibroes (Helsingor)
Carlsberg/Tuborg (Copenhagen)
Faxe Bryggeri (Fakse)

Sébastien Artois (Interbrew)
Grande Brasserie   (Armentières)
Moderne (Roubaix)
St Leonard (Lille)
Jeanne d'Arc (Ronchin)
Pelforth (Lille)
Lutèce (Paris)
Société Européene   Union de Brasseries (Paris)
(Sèvres)
Kronenbourg (Strasbourg)
FRANCE
SWITZERLAND
Cardinal (Fribourg)
Gurten (Bern)

LUXEMBOURG
Diekirch (Diekirch)
Mousel (Clausen)
Nationale (Bofferding)
Adelshoffen (Fischer) (Schiltigheim)
Pêcheur (Fischer) (Schiltigheim)
Météor (Hochfelden)
BräuAG (Linz)
Kuehtreiber (Hubertus) (Laa)
AUSTRIA
Ottakringer (Fassl) (Vienna)
Wieselburger (Wieselburg)
Gösser (Göss)
Puntigamer-Reininghaus (Graz)
Kärntner (Villach)
Stiegelbrauerei (Salzburg)
Adambrauerei (Innsbruck)
Schützengarten (St Gallen)
Calanda (Chur)
Haldengut (Winterthur)

Feldschlösschen (Rheinfelden)
Cardinal (Rheinfelden)

Hürlimann (Zurich)
Löwenbräu (Zurich)

See page 53 for map of Belgium.
See page 113 for map of Germany.
See page 147 for map of the Netherlands.
See page 124 for map of Ireland.
See page 153 for map of the United Kingdom.

TOP: Bofferding is the only brand of Luxembourg's Brasserie Nationale. ABOVE: Three brands from the portfolio of Mousel, Luxembourg's number two brewer. BELOW: Pripps is Sweden's leading brand. BOTTOM AND RIGHT: Ringnes of Oslo and Hansa of Bergen brew two of Norway's definitive lagers.

FACING PAGE: A brewery nightscape at the Brasserie Nationale in Bofferding, Luxembourg.

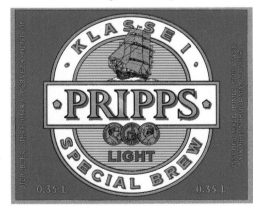

SWITZERLAND

In Belgium, they have King Gambrinus (Jan I or Jan Primus), but in Switzerland there is the legend of St Gall—an Irish monk whose name enters the literature as one of the many patron saints of brewing—who is said to have founded Switzerland's first brewery in the seventh century near the present-day city of St Gallen. St Gallen still has a major brewery—Schutzengarten AG on St Jakobstrasse—as do Basel (Warteck AG), Bern (Gurten AG), Chur (Calanda), Fribourg (Sibra), Luzern (Eichhof) and Winterthur (Haldengut). Like Germany and Austria, Switzerland is a nation of regional breweries rather than one dominant national brewer, as is the case in countries such as the Netherlands and Denmark. Zurich has two major brewers, Hürlimann and Löwenbräu Zurich, but the nation's largest is Feldschlösschen in Rheinfelden.

With labels bearing the distinctive long-tongued bear of Switzerland's capital canton, Gurten has been brewing in Wabern near Bern since Johann Juker first set up shop there in 1874. Calanda Haldengut traces its heritage to the Ernst family brewery in Winterthur in the early nineteenth century, but Johann Georg Schoolhorn, who entered the picture in 1875, is remembered as the man who put the brewery on the map.

Zurich's largest brewing company, Hürlimann, was founded in 1836 and has been brewing on the same site since 1866. Zurich's Löwenbräu (Lion's Brew) Brewery is occasionally confused with the more well-known Löwenbräu Brewery in Munich. The two are quite separate and the labels and colors quite different—except, of course, for the lion! St Gall *may* have first brewed beer at St Gallen in the seventh century, but Bräuerei Schutzengarten, the town brewery, *certainly* dates to 1779. Schutzengarten features the saint on one of its labels and a view of the brewery in the nineteenth century on its Festbier label. The company also brews Birell, a popular non-alcoholic beer.

TOP AND FACING PAGE, BOTTOM: Cardinal in Fribourg brews Cardinal lager and Anker, an altbier. ABOVE: Haldengut's Albani is a rich, dark beer. FACING PAGE, TOP: Schutzengarten's line includes the non-alcoholic Birell. FACING PAGE, SECOND ROW: Hürlimann's portfolio includes the dark and flavorful Hexenbräu (Witch's Brew) and Drei Konigs (Three Kings). RIGHT: Löwenbräu Zurich reverses its lion for the export market.

FESTBIER

Brauerei
Schützengarten

Mindestens haltbar bis

LAGER
BIER HELL

Schützengarten

58 cl
4,8% vol.

Helles Lagerbier aus feinem Malz
und edlem Hopfen, vom Braumeister
im Geschmack sorgfältig abgestimmt.

Mindestens haltbar bis

BRAUEREI SCHÜTZENGARTEN AG ST. GALLEN

7613 7020

DAS URECHTE BIER

BIRELL

BRAUEREI SCHÜTZENGARTEN AG
ST. GALLEN

Hergestellt nach Verfahren der Brauerei Hürlimann AG Zürich

Servire fresco

Kühl servieren

Servir frais

SANS ALCOOL · ALKOHOLFREI · ANALCOLICA

Mindestens haltbar bis

HEXEN
BRÄU

Sternstunden
aus der Zauberkraft,
die wunderbar
zufrieden macht.

Hürlimann

alc.
5.4 vol.%

Spezialbier dunkel.
Bière spéciale brune.

33 cl

mindestens haltbar bis
à consommer jusqu'au

LAGER
BIER

Das Bier mit Tradition.
Seit 1836.

Hürlimann

33 cl

mindestens haltbar bis
à consommer jusqu'au

alc.
4.8 vol.%

DREI-
KÖNIGS
BIER

Hürlimann

alc.
6.5 vol.%

Starkbier hell
Bière forte blonde

33 cl

mindestens haltbar bis
à consommer jusqu'au

LÖWENBRÄU

ZÜRICH

33 cl

Kühl servieren
Servir frais
Servire fresco

BIÈRE
SANS ALCOOL

BIER
ALKOHOLFREI

BIRRA
ANALCOLICA

Mindestens haltbar bis
à consommer de préférence avant le
Da consumarsi preferibilmente entro il

GERMANY

More than in Belgium or any other country on earth, the national drink of Germany is beer. Two out of every five breweries in the world are located in Germany. In terms of absolute production, Germany ranks second only to the United States. Even before unification, West Germany by itself was well ahead of third-place Britain. With nearly 1500 breweries—more than in all the world outside Europe combined—Germany has witnessed the evolution of a very robust industry.

With strong brewing companies in every region and state, Germany has no single dominant brand as do France, the Netherlands and Denmark. Bavaria is the largest brewing state in the Federal Republic and Dortmund in the state of Westphalia is Germany's largest brewing city.

With its size, the German brewing industry also offers a variety of brewing styles. Lagers are omnipresent, with Munich, Dortmund and Cologne (Köln) all having their own indigenous variations. Dusseldorf, a modern industrial city, is known as the home of altbier. Altbier, which literally means 'beer in the old style,' is brewed with top-fermenting (ale-type) yeast as all beers were before the lager revolution of the nineteenth century. Weissbiers (wheat beers) also predate lagers and are today brewed throughout Germany with specific styles indigenous to northern Germany, Bavaria and especially Berlin, where Berliner-Weisse is the city's trademark beer. Beck's lager is sent forth to the world from the port city of Bremen and is perhaps the biggest German export beer.

It was in the town of Krombach, in the state of Westphalia, where some of the first Pilsen-style lager was brewed. Today, Krombacher Pils is still brewed with water from the same pure mountain springs first developed in the eighteenth century. The brewery itself, Krombacher Bräuerei Bernhard Schadeberg, dates to 1802.

In the east, in the state of Saxony, the Sachsische Bräu Union (SBU) in Dresden was one of the largest government-owned brewing companies in the old East Germany (DDR). Today with an infusion of capital and technical expertise from Holsten in Hamburg, SBU is gearing up for the market economy.

As with many of North America's microbreweries, many German brewers offer a variety of styles, with most major brewers having light lagers (helles), dark lagers (dunkels), seasonal beers, (including märzenbiers), double bocks (doppelbocks) and wheat beers (weissbiers), to name but a few.

BELOW: The Krombacher Brewery in Westphalia as it appeared at the time of its centennial in 1902. FACING PAGE: The Hofbräuhaus in Munich is the world's most famous beer hall, a mecca for beer lovers everywhere.

BAVARIA AND SOUTHERN GERMANY

When it comes to beer, Bavaria is to Germany what Germany is to the world. A third of the world's breweries and 70 percent of Germany's breweries are in Bavaria, with breweries located in nearly every village. When it comes to superlatives, the state of Bavaria is to beer everything that its reputation implies.

Bavaria's capital, Munich, is one of the corners of lager brewing's Golden Triangle, as it was here that Gabriel Sedlmayr first developed a 'Munich-style' lager. Munich is also home to a big six—six of Germany's legendary brewing companies: Augustiner, Hacker-Pschorr, Löwenbräu, Paulaner, Spaten-Franziskaner and Hofbräuhaus (HB), whose Munich beer hall of the same name is the largest and most famous drinking establishment in the world.

'In Munich stands a Hofbräuhaus...' begin the words to the famous drinking song. Storied in song and prose (HL Mencken called it the Parthenon of beer drinking), the Hofbräuhaus beer hall can comfortably seat 4500, but often hosts more. The name literally means a royal beer hall

(hof), where beer is also brewed (bräuhaus)—rather like a brewpub except for the vast scale and imperial overtones. Today, however, the HB lagers are brewed off site, but the beer hall remains as perhaps the top tourist attraction in the city that likes to think of itself as the world capital of beer drinking.

Löwenbräu (*loven-broy* or Lion's Brew) in Munich brews what may be the best-known German beer brand in the world. Beck's in Bremen may export more beer, but Löwenbräu is license-brewed in Britain, Japan, the United States and other major beer-drinking countries. Löwenbräu began in 1383 as a Munich brewpub called Zum Löwen and evolved into a major lager brewery between 1826 and 1855. Paulaner dates back to the first beer brewed in 1631 by the monks of the order of St Francis of Paula. The monks sold their beer to the public after 1780, but the brewery became a secular lager brewery early in the nineteenth century. Today it is Munich's largest brewery, with an annual production approaching 1.6 million barrels (1.9 hectoliters).

FACING PAGE, TOP: Hofbräuhaus products celebrate the 'haus' itself, and include a special beer brewed for Munich's annual Oktoberfest, the world's premier beer event. FACING PAGE, ABOVE AND RIGHT: The Munich beer hall and product line of Löwenbräu. BELOW: Paulaner is Munich's largest brewing company.

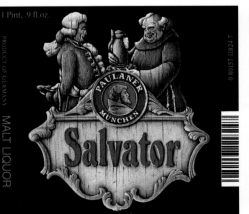

The beers of Spaten-Franziskaner represent the results of the 1922 merger of Gabriel Sedlmayr's Spaten Brewery and the Franziskaner (Franciscan) Brewery. The result is now one of Munich's big six brewing companies. Although the company traces its beginning to 1397, Spaten's true turning point occurred in the early nineteenth century when Sedlmayr became the first major Munich brewer to begin brewing large quantities of lager. As such, Sedlmayr played a pivotal role in the lager revolution and the development of the Munich style of lager. Today products include Spaten lagers as well as Franziskaner weissbiers.

Just outside Munich, the Ayinger Brewery traces its roots to 1878, when the Bavarian village of Aying had its first tavern brewery. Brewmaster Franz Insekammer is the sixth generation of his family to preside over the kettles at Ayinger.

Kulmbach is nestled in the rolling foothills of the Bavarian Alps in a picturesque town perched in a valley overlooked by a castle. The Erste Kulmbacher Union (EKU) is an amalgam of smaller breweries in the Kulmbach area that joined together in 1872 to brew Echt Kulmbacher Pils, which is still the EKU flagship beer. EKU also acquired Henninger of Frankfurt in 1987, and today both are part of the Maerz Group.

In addition to EKU, there are three breweries which may label their beers as a Kulmbacher beer. Reichelbräu AG owns and controls their own brewery, as well as the breweries of Sandlerbräu and Monchshof in Kulbach and Sternquell and Bräustolz in the former East Germany. Although owned by Reichelbräu, each of the breweries are separate entities. Each is run by a different individual brewmaster, who produces the beers that in his judgment are the finest possible using all the skill and knowledge he can command. Each brewery's beer product is different in taste, color, and in many cases, alcohol content.

In 1846, Reichelbräu AG became the name of the present brewery and has been in continuous operation for 139 years. Its Edelherb Pils and Edelkulm are positioned as premium beers. Prior to 1982, Reichelbräu was sold in two markets, Germany and Italy. In 1982, it was introduced into the United States and later was sold worldwide in Australia, China and Japan, as well as Hungary, Poland and the Czech Republic. All Reichelbräu beers are produced by the bottom-fermentation process and are aged (lagered).

Established in Bamberg in 1718, Kaiserdom is world famous for its rauchbier. Indigenous to that area of southern Germany centered on Bamberg, rauchbier is literally

ABOVE AND BELOW: The architecturally striking, modern Kulmbach brewhouse; and part of the product line of Erste Kulmbacher Union (EKU). RIGHT: The beers of the Ayinger Brewery in Aying near Munich. The label illustrations celebrate rural life.

FACING PAGE: The brewery and flagship lager (seen here in export packaging) of Munich's Spaten brewery. The initials in the 'spade' logo are those of Spaten's Gabriel Sedlmayer, who is credited with having invented the Munich style of lager in about the 1830s.

'smoked beer.' The malted grain used in the brewing of rauchbier is roasted over a beechwood fire. As such, the grain is not only roasted to a dark color, but it takes on a distinctive smoky flavor as well. Smoked beer, which is rare outside of Germany, is generally served with meals including smoked or barbecued meats, rye bread and certain sharp cheeses.

Another unique and extraordinary beer from Bavaria is steinbiere (stone-brewed beer). It is brewed at the Rauchenfels Brewery in Marktoberdorf, which also produces both light and dark hefeweiss. For many centuries, heated stones were the only method of heating large quantities of liquid. Stone-brewed beers were most often produced in the Alpine region, where the special stones needed for the brewing process could be easily quarried. For brewers, this method made it possible to brew a top-fermented beer with a special flavor. When large breweries were built in the nineteenth century, the tedious process of making stone-brewed beers became completely forgotten until

Rauchenfels revised the process. In this process, stones are heated to 1200 degrees C (650 degrees F) over a beechwood fire and then dropped into the brew kettles. The result is a beer which, like rauchbier, has a unique, smoky flavor.

Adjacent to Bavaria is the state of Baden Wurtenberg, whose principle city is Stuttgart. Dinkelacker, Stuttgart's leading brewery, was founded by Carl Dinkelacker in 1888. The product line includes Cluss, a keller-style lager, and Leicht, a low-calorie beer introduced in 1990. Stuttgart's Schwaben Bräu Robert Leicht AG evolved from the first beer brewed in 1878 by Robert Leicht at his gasthof (guest house) called Ochsen.

Located in Donaueschingen near the source of the Danube, the Fürstenberg Brewery dates from a 1283 charter issued by Rudolf von Hapsburg, and in 1895 Fürstenberg's brewmaster, Josef Munz, was declared by Kaiser Wilhelm II to be the premier brewer of the Pilsen-style lager in Germany. Today, Fürstenberg brews pilsners as well as alcohol-free pilsners.

ABOVE AND FACING PAGE, BOTTOM: One of Stuttgart's three major brewers, Schwabenbräu is noted for its pilsener. RIGHT: Founded in 1888 by the family of the same name, Dinkelacker is the biggest brewer in Stuttgart. FACING PAGE: Some of the other interesting beers of Germany's south include those brewed by Fürstenberg, Franz Joseph Sailer (Oberdorfer) of Marktoberdorf, Cluss of Heilbronn and Kaiserdom of Bamberg. BELOW: Kaiserdom Rauchbier is an extraordinary delight to the palate in the company of such foods.

DORTMUND

Dortmund is Germany's largest brewing city, with the giant Dortmunder Actien Bräuerei (DAB) and the rival Dortmunder Union Bräuerei (DUB) located there. The brewing tradition of Dortmund began in 1293 and progressed into the nineteenth century when Dortmunder bottom-fermented beers became popular. Dortmunder lagers are traditionally full-bodied but not quite as sweet as the beers of Munich, though not as dry as a true pilsner. This style evolved when they began transporting beer to other markets across the continent. In order to withstand the rigors of travel, Dortmund brewers produced a beer that was well hopped and slightly higher in alcohol. As such, the Dortmund lager as a style is known as 'export.' Beers identified as such are not necessarily brewed specifically to be exported, although they often are.

The Dortmunder Union Bräuerei (DUB) was formed in 1873 by the merger of several small breweries, and has been ranked among the top 10 German breweries since 1939. Because of its location in the heavily bombed industrial Ruhr, the brewery was 75 percent destroyed in World War II. It was rebuilt and enjoyed continuous growth until 1972, when it merged with two other brewing groups and became the Dortmunder Union Schultheiss Bräuerei. DUB is now part of Bräu und Brunnen AG, the largest beverage group in Germany. The leading breweries within Bräu und Brunnen are: DUB; Dortmunder Ritter, located in Dortmund; Heidelberger Schlossguell Bräuerei (home of the famous Valentins Weizen Beer) in Heidelberg; Schultheiss Bräuerei, the largest brewery in Berlin; and Einbecker Bräu Haus in Einbeck, the oldest bock beer brewery in Germany.

ABOVE: The original 'export' lager from Dortmunder Union (DUB). Dortmund is noted for its export-style lager, which is generally similar to a classic pilsener. BELOW: DUB is a sister company to Berlin's Schultheiss and Einbeck's Einbecker. Einbecker's is the oldest bock beer brand in the country. Martin Luther allegedly drank it. BELOW RIGHT: Dortmund's DAB is the biggest brewer in Germany's biggest brewing city.

MAJOR BREWERIES OF GERMANY

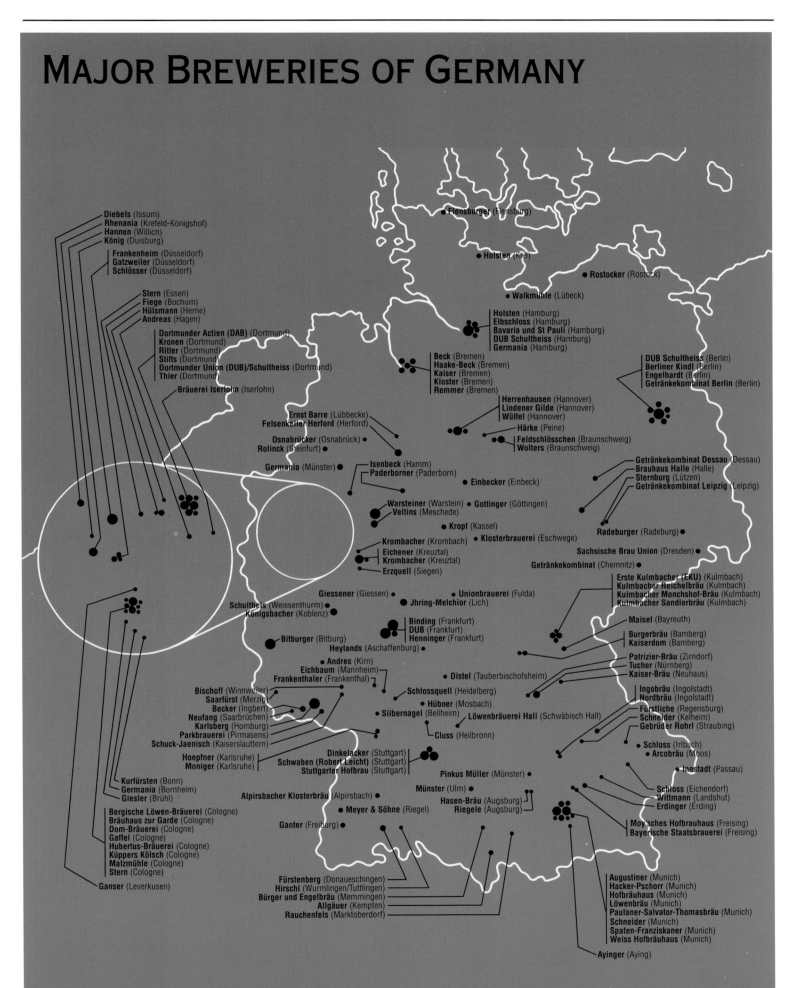

Diebels (Issum)
Rhenania (Krefeld-Königshof)
Hannen (Willich)
König (Duisburg)

Frankenheim (Düsseldorf)
Gatzweiler (Düsseldorf)
Schlösser (Düsseldorf)

Stern (Essen)
Fiege (Bochum)
Hülsmann (Herne)
Andreas (Hagen)

Dortmunder Actien (DAB) (Dortmund)
Kronen (Dortmund)
Ritter (Dortmund)
Stifts (Dortmund)
Dortmunder Union (DUB)/Schultheiss (Dortmund)
Thier (Dortmund)

Bräuerei Iserlohn (Iserlohn)

Ernst Barre (Lübbecke)
Felsenkeller Herford (Herford)

Osnabrücker (Osnabrück)
Rolinck (Steinfurt)

Germania (Münster)

Isenbeck (Hamm)
Paderborner (Paderborn)

Warsteiner (Warstein)
Veltins (Meschede)

Krombacher (Krombach)
Eichener (Kreuztal)
Krombacher (Kreuztal)
Erzquell (Siegen)

Giessener (Giessen)
Schultheis (Weissenthurm)
Königsbacher (Koblenz)

Bitburger (Bitburg)
Heylands (Aschaffenburg)

Andres (Kirn)
Eichbaum (Mannheim)
Frankenthaler (Frankenthal)

Bischoff (Winnweiler)
Saarfürst (Merzig)
Becker (Ingbert)
Neufang (Saarbrücken)
Karlsberg (Homburg)
Parkbrauerei (Pirmasens)
Schuck-Jaenisch (Kaiserslautern)

Hoepfner (Karlsruhe)
Moniger (Karlsruhe)

Kurfürsten (Bonn)
Germania (Bornheim)
Giesler (Brühl)

Bergische Löwen-Bräuerei (Cologne)
Bräuhaus zur Garde (Cologne)
Dom-Bräuerei (Cologne)
Gaffel (Cologne)
Hubertus-Bräuerei (Cologne)
Küppers Kölsch (Cologne)
Malzmühle (Cologne)
Stern (Cologne)

Ganser (Leverkusen)

Flensburger (Flensburg)

Holsten (Kiel)

Rostocker (Rostock)

Walkmühle (Lübeck)

Holsten (Hamburg)
Elbschloss (Hamburg)
Bavaria und St Pauli (Hamburg)
DUB Schultheiss (Hamburg)
Germania (Hamburg)

Beck (Bremen)
Haake-Beck (Bremen)
Kaiser (Bremen)
Kloster (Bremen)
Remmer (Bremen)

Herrenhausen (Hannover)
Lindener Gilde (Hannover)
Wülfel (Hannover)

Härke (Peine)

Feldschlösschen (Braunschweig)
Wolters (Braunschweig)

Einbecker (Einbeck)

Gottinger (Göttingen)

Kropf (Kassel)

Klosterbrauerei (Eschwege)

Unionbrauerei (Fulda)
Jhring-Melchior (Lich)

Binding (Frankfurt)
DUB (Frankfurt)
Henninger (Frankfurt)

Distel (Tauberbischofsheim)

Schlossquell (Heidelberg)
Hübner (Mosbach)
Silbernagel (Bellheim)
Löwenbräuerei Hall (Schwäbisch Hall)
Cluss (Heilbronn)

Dinkelacker (Stuttgart)
Schwaben (Robert Leicht) (Stuttgart)
Stuttgarter Hofbrau (Stuttgart)

Pinkus Müller (Münster)

Münster (Ulm)

Hasen-Bräu (Augsburg)
Riegele (Augsburg)

Alpirsbacher Klosterbräu (Alpirsbach)

Meyer & Söhne (Riegel)

Ganter (Freiburg)

DUB Schultheiss (Berlin)
Berliner Kindl (Berlin)
Engelhardt (Berlin)
Getränkekombinat Berlin (Berlin)

Getränkekombinat Dessau (Dessau)
Brauhaus Halle (Halle)
Sternburg (Lützen)
Getränkekombinat Leipzig (Leipzig)

Radeburger (Radeburg)

Sachsische Brau Union (Dresden)

Getränkekombinat (Chemnitz)

Erste Kulmbacher (EKU) (Kulmbach)
Kulmbacher Reichelbräu (Kulmbach)
Kulmbacher Monchshof-Bräu (Kulmbach)
Kulmbacher Sandlerbräu (Kulmbach)

Maisel (Bayreuth)

Burgerbräu (Bamberg)
Kaiserdom (Bamberg)

Patrizier-Bräu (Zirndorf)
Tucher (Nürnberg)
Kaiser-Bräu (Neuhaus)

Ingobräu (Ingolstadt)
Nordbräu (Ingolstadt)
Fürstliche (Regensburg)
Schneider (Kelheim)
Gebrüder Rohrl (Straubing)

Schloss (Irlbach)
Arcobräu (Moos)

Innstadt (Passau)

Schloss (Eichendorf)
Wittmann (Landshut)
Erdinger (Erding)

Moy'sches Hofbrauhaus (Freising)
Bayerische Staatsbrauerei (Freising)

Fürstenberg (Donaueschingen)
Hirschi (Wurmlingen/Tuttlingen)
Bürger und Engelbräu (Memmingen)
Allgäuer (Kempten)
Rauchenfels (Marktoberdorf)

Augustiner (Munich)
Hacker-Pschorr (Munich)
Hofbräuhaus (Munich)
Löwenbräu (Munich)
Paulaner-Salvator-Thomasbräu (Munich)
Schneider (Munich)
Spaten-Franziskaner (Munich)
Weiss Hofbräuhaus (Munich)

Ayinger (Aying)

RHINELAND AND ADJACENT AREAS

A traveler to the valleys of Germany's legendary Rhine and Moselle rivers will quickly notice that the distinctive logotype of Bitburger Bräuerei Theobold Simon is a ubiquitous sight in the towns and cities of this region from Trier to Bonn to Frankfurt. The Bitburger name is also known in 24 countries throughout Europe, as well as in North America and the Far East. The brewery was founded at Bitburg near Trier in 1817 by Johann Peter Wallenborn. His original objective was simply to produce altbier for his own pub. In 1876, however, his grandson Theobold Simon began an aggressive marketing plan, and in 1884 he switched from alt to lager and Bitburger Pils was born. The brewery reached the 840,000-barrel (one-million-hectoliter) production level in 1973 and doubled that output in the next 10 years, making it one of Germany's leading national brands. Begun in 1869 by Christian Henninger, one of Frankfurt's best-known brewing companies, Henninger also has a strong market presence in the Mediterranean. Although the company was acquired by EKU in 1987, Henninger retains a separate marketing identity. Meanwhile, the Binding Brewery of Frankfurt is noted for its highly successful Clausthaler non-alcoholic beer, along with other products.

Just as Dortmund has given the name 'export' to its own distinctive variation on the lager style, the city of Cologne (Köln) has given its name to a top-fermented beer. Although Dusseldorf, halfway between Cologne and Dortmund, is the spiritual home of altbier, Cologne is famous for its Kölsch, which is fermented with alt yeast but has the lighter, golden color of a pilsner or an export. The Bräuerei zur Malzmuhle (Malt Mill) in Cologne brews a low-alcohol lager called Kochsches Malzbier, as well as Mühlen Kölsch (The Windmill of Cologne) beers.

ABOVE: Bitburger Pils is a characteristic interpretation of the classic international pilsener style. RIGHT: Henninger, one of Frankfurt's two major brewers, soars to advertise. BELOW AND FACING PAGE, BOTTOM: Soaring over Frankfurt, one might wish to set down on the Binding Brewery's logo. A pilot could afford to have a drink here, as Binding's major export product is Clausthaler non-alcoholic beer. FACING PAGE, TOP: Two interpretations of Cologne's Kölsch, which looks like a pilsener, but is fermented like altbier.

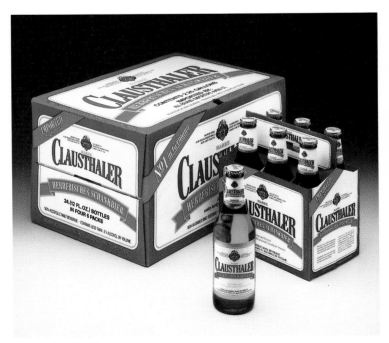

NORTHERN GERMANY

The city-state of Bremen has been an important seaport since the days of the Hanseatic League more than 600 years ago. With this in mind, it is little wonder that the lagers of Bräuerei Beck & Company have become Germany's leading export brand. Beck's beers are found not only throughout Europe but on every continent.

Two other important brewing centers in the north of Germany are the city-state of Hamburg and Hanover in Niedersachsen. It was in 1526, when a brewer named Cord Broyhan brewed his first beer in Hanover. Two decades later, the Hanover Brewers Guild (Gilde) was founded, taking as its symbol a seal with Broyhan's initial. The Guild's brewery evolved over the centuries, and in 1968, it took over the 114-year-old Lindener Aktien-Bräuerei, which markets its products under the name Lindener-Gilde. Another important beer in northern Germany—and even more important in the export market—is Holsten, which was founded in 1879 at Altona (now part of Hamburg). In 1952, Holsten brewing plants at Hamburg, Kiel and Neumunster had exceeded 250,000 barrels (297,000 hectoliters), and by the 1990s, Holsten was brewing over 700,000 barrels (833,000 hectoliters) annually. Another Hamburg brewery that is important to the export market is St Pauli, whose 'St Pauli Girl' is a popular icon.

The Holsten Group, which developed from the Holsten Bräuerei AG, is one of the biggest brewery groups in Germany, with breweries in Hamburg and Kiel, the Feldschlösschen Brewery in Braunschweig, the Kronen Brewery in Luneberg, the Mecklenburg Brewery in Lubz and the Sachsische Bräu-Union AG in Dresden in the former East Germany. By the early 1990s, Holsten's volume increased to 795,000 barrels (1.3 million hectoliters) and sales were increasing by over 10 percent annually. Meanwhile, Holsten beer was produced under license in breweries in Great Britain, China, Nigeria, Hungary and, since 1992 in Namibia.

TOP RIGHT: The Feldschlösschen Brewery in Braunschweig. During the 45 years that Germany was divided, a state-owned Feldschlösschen Brewery also existed in Dresden in East Germany. Today both are part of the Holsten Group. RIGHT: From these great kettles come the beers of Beck's, Germany's most exported brand. The anchors in the stained-glass window symbolize the importance that Beck's attached to international trade.

ABOVE: Because Bremen is an important seaport, the beers brewed here have become well-known abroad. RIGHT: Beers of Hamburg also enjoy proximity to a seaport and are known abroad, especially in America and the UK. TOP RIGHT: Gilde brews altbier as well as the Pilsener seen here. BELOW: Brewed in Braunschweig, Feldschlösschen has a cousin in Dresden.

ALTBIER

Altbier is the German equivalent of English or American ale, literally a beer made in the 'old' way (pre-nineteenth century) with top-fermenting yeast. It is indigenous to Dusseldorf and its environs.

Characteristic of 'alt brewers' is the Gatzweiler family, which has been brewing altbier since 1313, and operated the Zum Schlüssel Haus Bräuerei (a brewpub) in Dusseldorf from 1937 to 1944 until it was destroyed in World War II. Zum Schlüssel was rebuilt after the war and was augmented by the construction of a large, modern brewery in 1963. The traditional altbier line was expanded in 1988 by the introduction of the non-alcoholic alt Gatz Alkoholfrei.

Another alt brewery is the Bräuerei Schlosser, which is located in the heart of Dusseldorf's *altstadt* ('old city'), the mecca for those interested in altbier. Schlosser is now part of the Dortmunder Union (DUB) Group.

As noted above, the area round Dusseldorf (and including Duisberg) is the spiritual home of altbier as a style. 'Diebels, das freundliche (friendly) Alt' reads the slogan for Germany's largest selling altbier, which is brewed in the small town of Issum on the lower Rhine near Dusseldorf. Diebels has also marketed a highly successful non-alcoholic altbier, Issumr Alkoholfrei, since 1987, and a light beer, Diebels Light, since April 1992. Josef Diebels wrote to the mayor of Issum on 31 August 1877 requesting permission to start a brewery. The rest is history. In 1981, Diebels reached an annual production of 840,000 barrels (one million hectoliters). Today Dr Paul Boesken-Diebels, a great-grandson of the brewery's founder, is the chief executive officer.

Another altbier of note is brewed in Münster by the hausbräueri of Pinkus Müller, which dates to 1816. Founded by Johannes Müller, the brewery is named for fourth gen-

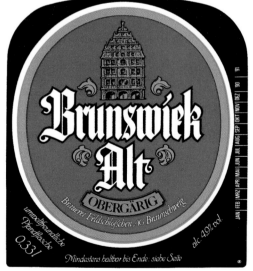

eration Carl Pinkus Müller, who was its guiding light until his death in 1979. Pinkus was known as 'the singing brewer' for his public appearances, as well as his impromptu seranades around the brewhouse. Professionally trained as a vocalist, Pinkus is perhaps best remembered for his New Years Eve 1963 role in Mozart's *Die Fledermaus* in Münster.

RIGHT AND BOTTOM RIGHT: The brewpub known as Zum Schlüssel (Key) has been pleasing patrons with altbier since 1937, whereas the hosts, the Gatzweilers, have been brewing since 1313. They now bottle their beer. BELOW: A selection of altbiers from Berlin, Munster, Hesse and Dusseldorf. FACING PAGE: Diebels of Issum (near Dusseldorf) calls itself the 'friendly alt' and is the biggest selling brewer of altbier. FACING PAGE, BOTTOM: Feldschlösschen of Braunschweig (Brunswick) is one of many brewers outside of the Dusseldorf area to brew altbier.

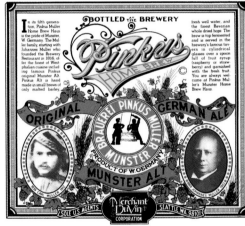

WEISSBIER

Weissbier is a German word literally meaning beer that is white (weiss), but actually implying a style of pale-colored, top-fermented beer made with about half wheat malt. Beer, by definition, is a beverage derived from malted barley. Other grains, such as rice and cornmeal, are often used in less expensive, mass market brands as a cheaper source of starch, but this practice is frowned upon by discriminating brewers and consumers. Exceptions are made in the case of oats in English oatmeal stout and in American wheat beer, German weissbier and Flemish witbier. Both the German and Flemish terms are literally translated as meaning 'white beer.' This is a reference to the light color of the beer and the fact that it usually has yeast particles in suspension and hence it is cloudy, translucent and lighter in appearance than if it were transparent. In Germany weissbeirs which are cloudy are identified with the prefix *hefe* (yeast) as hefeweissbier, or simply hefeweiss. Weissbier is also known as weizenbier, but should not be confused with wiesenbier, which is a festival beer that may or may not contain wheat malt.

During the seventeenth and eighteenth centuries, weissbier had been tremendously popular in Germany. However, by the time that Georg Schneider took over the Weiss Hofbräuhaus in Munich in 1872, weissbier had been suffering a dramatic loss of market share to lager. Schneider sought to re-establish the popularity of the style in Bavaria, and succeeded. In 1928, the old weissbräuhaus in Kelheim on the Danube was also acquired and many of the important weiss breweries of the seventeenth and eighteenth centuries were under the same umbrella. Just as Munich, Dortmund and Dusseldorf all have indigenous local beer styles, so too does Germany's long divided capital, Berlin. Berliner-Weiss is a particularly pale hefeweiss noted for its fruitiness, which has been very popular—served in champagne glasses—in Berlin's café scene since the early nineteenth century. Both of Berlin's major brewing companies, Kindl and Schultheiss, produce Berliner-Weiss—on both sides of the former Berlin wall—as well as other beers.

CLOCKWISE FROM BELOW: Selected weissbiers from around Germany include Maisels from Bayreuth, Franziskaner from Spaten-Franziskaner in Munich, Schneider from Munich, Berliner Kindl from Berlin and Münchner Kindl from Hofbräuhaus in Munich.

IRELAND

Brewing originated in Ireland in ancient times. Barley was cultivated here as early as 3000 BC and St Patrick himself is said to have employed a brewer. The Greek scholar Dioscorides, writing in the first century, noted that the Irish drank *curmi*, a fermented beverage made with malted barley flavored with herbs. The *Seanchus Mor* of 441 AD states that barley was cultivated only for brewing.

It has been recorded that in the north of Ireland during the ninth century, beer was brewed from heath. Actually honey, and the flower of the heath, were used as a substitute for hops. Indeed, before the introduction of hops, broom tops, wormwood and other bitter herbs had been employed as seasonings. Wormus spoke of the drinking of heather beer as one of the pleasures which the souls of departed heroes enjoyed in the society of the gods. There was also a story of a man in the eighteenth century who tried to manufacture a heather beer in County Donegal, but he did not find that it pleased the palates of his friends, who had long been accustomed to bayberries and ivy berries, which were themselves sorry enough substitutes for hops.

According to the *Annals of Ulster* (1107 AD), the Irish also had another beverage, a mixture of water and honey now called mead but then called *miodh* or *mil-fion* (honey-wine). This reference also appears in the life of St Berach, who flourished in the seventh century.

By the end of the twelfth century, a considerable volume of ale was already being brewed in Dublin along the course of the Poddle River, whose waters are considered ideal for the purpose. Writing in 1610, Barnaby Rych in his *New Description of Ireland* (1610) gave an account of the brewing industry in Dublin during the reign of James I and

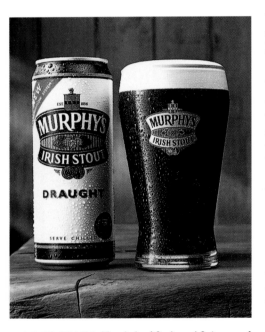

ABOVE AND OPPOSITE: Murphy's of Cork, and Guinness of Dublin are Ireland's biggest producers of stout.

Charles II. By that time, he estimated that there were 1180 ale houses and 91 brewpubs in the city of Dublin, whose population was only 4000 families. During the eighteenth century, however, the brewing of beer passed gradually from the hands of small pub brewers and home brewers to those of commercial brewers, who had first been incorporated in Dublin by Royal Charter in 1696.

Over the years, Ireland developed an indigenous beer style that was extremely popular at home and exported successfully throughout the world, but which was *brewed* almost nowhere else in the world. Today, just as the beer style in the United Kingdom is ale, Ireland is the only nation where the primary beer style is stout. Like ale, stout is produced with top-fermenting yeast. However, it derives its nearly black color from the

barley and barley malt used in the brewing process, which is roasted until it is a very dark brown.

The major brewer of stout in Ireland, and indeed in the world, is Arthur Guinness & Sons of Dublin. The other major Irish brewing companies—Murphy and Beamish—are also stout brewers and they are both located in Cork, the Republic of Ireland's second largest city. Guinness is brewed throughout the world, but primarily in London, England, and at the flagship St James' Gate Brewery in Dublin. The actual St James' Gate was the ancient entrance to the outer city from the suburbs of Dublin. It can be seen on Speed's map of Dublin (1610) and on Brooking's map of Dublin (1728), and it was very near to where the main gate of the Guinness Brewery is now situated. The area of the city of Dublin adjacent to St James' Gate had, from very early times, been a favorite neighborhood for breweries, because it lay on the main road to the capital from the grain-growing districts of central Ireland. The primary supply of water to the city, derived from the Poddle River, also passed through the area before entering the city proper.

The first brewery was established at St James' Gate in 1670 by Giles Mee, who obtained a lease from the Municipal Corporation entitling him to certain water rights described as the 'ground called the pipes in the parish of St James', and these rights eventually passed into the ownership of Sir Mark Rainsford, brewer, of St James' Gate. Documents preserved in the Public Registry of Deeds, Dublin, record that in 1693 alderman Sir Mark Rainsford had a brewhouse at St James' Gate where 'beer and fine ales' were made.

In November 1715, Rainsford apparently went out of business and the lease was then granted for 99 years to Paul Espinasse. The

MAJOR BREWERIES OF IRELAND

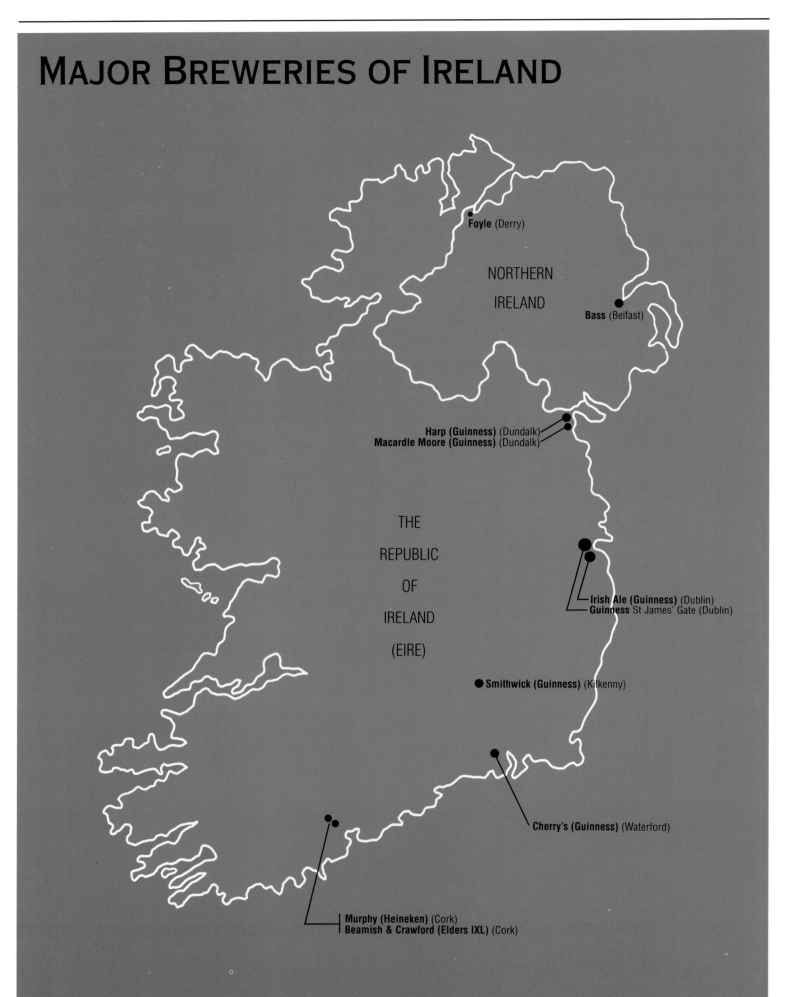

Foyle (Derry)

NORTHERN

IRELAND

Bass (Belfast)

Harp (Guinness) (Dundalk)
Macardle Moore (Guinness) (Dundalk)

THE

REPUBLIC

OF

IRELAND

(EIRE)

Irish Ale (Guinness) (Dublin)
Guinness St James' Gate (Dublin)

● **Smithwick (Guinness)** (Kilkenny)

Cherry's (Guinness) (Waterford)

Murphy (Heineken) (Cork)
Beamish & Crawford (Elders IXL) (Cork)

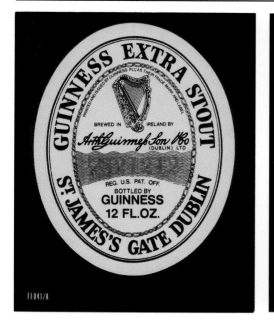

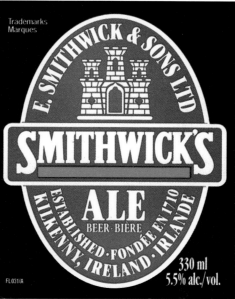

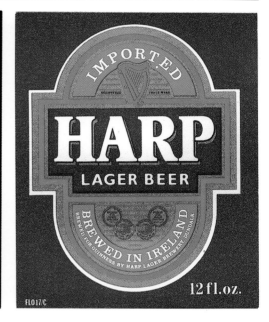

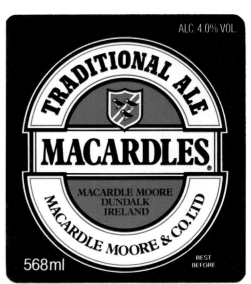

Espinasse family carried on the brewing business until December 1759, when the brewery was leased by Mark Rainsford of Portarlinton (Sir Mark Rainsford's son) to Arthur Guinness of the City of Dublin for 9000 years, to be held 'in as ample and beneficial a manner as the same were formerly held by Paul Espinasse or John Espinasse' at a rent of 45 pounds per year. Born in 1725, Arthur Guinness was the eldest son of Richard Guinness of Celbridge, County Kildare, who was an agent and receiver for Dr Arthur Price.

Ireland was at that time occupied by the British, who sought to protect and promote the sale of their own products into Ireland. Amazingly, the duty on beer imported from England was merely a fraction of a shilling per barrel, while that brewed within Ireland was taxed at five shillings per barrel. Ireland could hardly hope to compete with imported beer under such circumstances. In spite of this, Arthur Guinness struggled on and became successful, especially after 1782 when the legislative independence of Ireland was established by the British Parliament.

Henry Gratton, who later supported the Dublin brewers before the Irish Parliament, wrote to Arthur Guinness that he regarded St James' Gate Brewery as 'the actual nurse of the people, entitled to every encouragement.'

When Arthur Guinness died in 1803 at the age of 78, the brewery passed to Arthur, Benjamin and William Lunell Guinness, his second, fourth and fifth sons. Benjamin died in 1826 and William Lunell in 1842. At that time, the business became vested in their elder brother, Arthur Guinness, who died in 1855. In about 1858, the sole ownership of the brewery went to Benjamin Lee Guinness, Arthur's third son. Sir Benjamin died in 1868, leaving the brewery to his eldest and

third sons, Arthur III and Edward Cecil (later lords Ardilaun and Iveagh). In 1876, Arthur sold his half-share to his brother Edward, and in 1886 the undertaking was turned into a limited company and sold to the public for £6 million.

From that date, Guinness went on to capture the Irish and London markets—and eventually the markets of the world. During the early decades of the twentieth century, the St James' Gate Brewery in Dublin was the largest brewery in the world, and, although it has since been surpassed, it is still one of the world's major brewing centers.

As a beverage, Guinness Stout is legendary, with a worldwide following whose enthusiasm is unrivaled by that of any other drink. A British cavalry officer, wounded at Waterloo in 1815, wrote in his diary as he lay in the hospital, 'When I was sufficiently recovered to be permitted to take some nourishment I felt the most extraordinary desire for a glass of Guinness. . . I shall never forget how much I enjoyed it. I thought I had never tasted anything so delightful.'

Benjamin Disraeli, the former prime minister of England, wrote to his sister Sarah on 21 November 1837, '. . . There was a division on the address in Queen Victoria's first Parliament—509 to 20. . . I then left the House at 10 o'clock, none of us having dined. The tumult and excitement [was] great... I supped at the Carlton, with a large party, of oysters and Guinness, and got to bed at halfpast 12 o'clock. Thus ended the most remarkable day hitherto of my life.'

While Guinness clearly dominates the brewing scene in the capital, the city of Cork has always been considered an excellent location for a brewery because the fine malting barley from the nearby limestone soils was combined with the pure water of the city. Ireland's number two brewing com-

ABOVE FROM TOP LEFT: The brands of Arthur Guinness & Son include the flagship beer brewed at St James' Gate Brewery in Dublin, as well as regional subsidiaries at Kilkenny, Dundalk and Waterford. The brewing styles range from the famous stout to pale ales to lagers. Harp Lager is second only to Guinness Stout in popularity abroad.

pany, James J Murphy & Company, Ltd, was founded in 1856 at Lady's Well in Cork by the four Murphy brothers, James, William, Jerome and Francis. The name is derived from a celebrated well on the hill opposite the brewery which was dedicated to the Virgin Mary and which is believed to possess miraculous properties. Pilgrims make their way to the shrine each year in May. In the nineteenth century, Lady's Well was one of Cork's largest breweries. Initially, Murphy's Brewery brewed porter but switched to stout, which it has brewed ever since. In 1975,

James J Murphy signed a licensing agreement with the Netherlands' largest brewing company to brew Heineken for the Irish market, and a marketing company, called Heineken Ireland, Ltd, was set up. In 1983, the firm was purchased by Heineken International, which immediately initiated a huge investment by building a new brewery on the same site as the old plant. Murphy's Irish Stout was relaunched with a new label, and is now exported and promoted at home and abroad using Heineken's international marketing expertise.

Beamish & Crawford began in January 1792 as a partnership between William Beamish, William Crawford, Richard Barrett and Digby O'Brien. In their agreement, Barrett and O'Brien were described as brewers and Beamish and Crawford as merchants. The partnership was to be known as the Cork Porter Brewery. The partners rented a brewery at Cramer's Lane, which forms part of the present brewery site, from Edward Allen, whose father, Aylmer Allen, had been brewing there since 1715. (There is evidence of a brewery on the site since 1600.)

THESE PAGES: Cork's two major stout brewers have been cross-town rivals since the brothers Murphy started brewing at Lady's Well in 1856. Both brands are now well-known to the export market.

The partnership prospered from the start, and by 1805 the annual production constituted over two-thirds of the total production of the nine breweries that existed in Cork at the time. O'Brien died and Barrett retired from the business before 1800, and the Beamish and Crawford families carried on the business successfully from the beginning of the nineteenth century. Indeed, the firm was the largest brewery in Ireland during the first half of the nineteenth century.

In 1901, the present Beamish & Crawford Company was formed and took over the neighboring Southgate Brewery of Lane & Company, which had been founded in 1758. In 1906, St Stephen's Brewery at Dungarvan was purchased and the Bandon Brewing Company of Allman, Dowden & Company became part of the company in 1914. In turn, Beamish & Crawford itself was purchased by Canadian Breweries Ltd (Later Carling O'Keefe Ltd) in 1962. A complete modernization of the brewery began in 1963, although the Elizabethan style and character of the South Main Street facade was retained. The brewing of Carling's Black Label lager in Cork began in 1964.

In 1987, Elders IXL of Australia, then the fourth largest brewing company in the world, took over Carling O'Keefe and hence the Cork-based brewery as well. This takeover led to the introduction to the Irish market of Foster's Lager. At the same time, Elders also acquired Courage in England, and today Beamish Stout is widely available in Britain through the Courage pubs, along with the 12 regional brewers who distribute Courage.

LATIN AMERICA
AND THE
CARIBBEAN

As in the ancient Middle East 5000 years ago and China 3000 years ago, the Americas had a brewing tradition that predated the arrival of European beer. An indigenous native 'black' beer was brewed in Brazil in pre-Columbian times (before 1492) and is still brewed in remote corners of the Upper Amazon. It took its name from its color, which is derived from grain that is roasted until it is a very dark brown, not unlike that used for an Irish stout. The purest form of this unique native-style brew that is available in the outside world is Xingu (*shin-gu*), named for a tributary of the Amazon River. The beer was 'discovered' and nurtured for export by Alan Eames, the noted beer anthropologist. It is now brewed in export quantities at Cacador, Brazil, by Cervejaria Cacador.

Meanwhile, the Mayan-speaking peoples of pre-Columbian Central America favored a beer made of fermented cornstalks, while the Uto-Aztecans and others (such as the Pueblo and Tarahumar) of northern Mexico and the border country brewed a sprouted maize beer. Known as *Tesguino* or *Tiswin*, this beer was produced in a manner that is more reminiscent of familiar brewing processes. For the tribes of the Yucatan peninsula, such as the Maya, corn and corn products were the central focus of their lifestyle, from food to religion.

The first Spanish breweries (*cervecería*) were established in the 1500s, but in the ensuing three centuries Latin American tastes paralleled those of Spain, just as North American tastes paralleled those of England. This meant an inclination toward wine and

distilled spirits, such as mescal and tequila rather than beer (*cerveza*). There was also *pulque*, a fermented beverage favored in the nineteenth century by peasants. The climate of much of Latin America prevented the brewing of lager until the latter part of the century when artificial ice-making became widely practiced. Early breweries were relatively small and brewed *sencilla* or *corriente* beer, which was similar to lager but fermented for a shorter period of time.

BELOW: Cervecería Central was acquired by Cuauhtémoc, which merged with Moctezuma in 1985 to form Valores, Mexico's largest brewer. Moctezuma brews Dos Equis (FACING PAGE), a popular amber lager.

The first European-style brewery in the New World was granted as a concession by Don Antonio de Mendoz in Mexico on 12 December 1543 to Don Alonso de Herrera, who was 'born in the city of Seville, a legitimate son of Pedro Herrera and Isabel de Baeca, who later went to the New Spain some 24 years ago with his arms and horse.'

The brewery was constructed in 1544 with formal permission issued in 1554 by Don Luis de Velàsco who stated, 'In view of the fact that you have complied with that which was stated, you now have begun the brewing of beer, and you have brewed beer in the city of Mexico. You have sold it and are presently selling the stated *zerbeza* (desire).'

Don Alonso's promotion of beer consumption was so strong that in a letter addressed to the emperor he affirmed, with the vision of a progressive entrepreneur, that some 100 brewing vats could be installed in view of the great extension of land available and the increase of the population, and that each of the aforementioned vats could increase the royal treasury by some 1000 pesos a year.

There was an influx of German immigrants in the mid-nineteenth century and this opened the door for lager brewing. The first Mexican brewery of modern times, Pila-Seca, was founded in Mexico City prior to 1845 by Swiss immigrant Bernherd Bolgard, who brewed with sun-dried barley, which was mixed with molasses. A contemporary of Pila-Seca was La Candelria, owned by the Bavarian Federico Herzog. In 1860, Carlos Fredenbaen founded the San Diego Brewery, which continued operation until 1889.

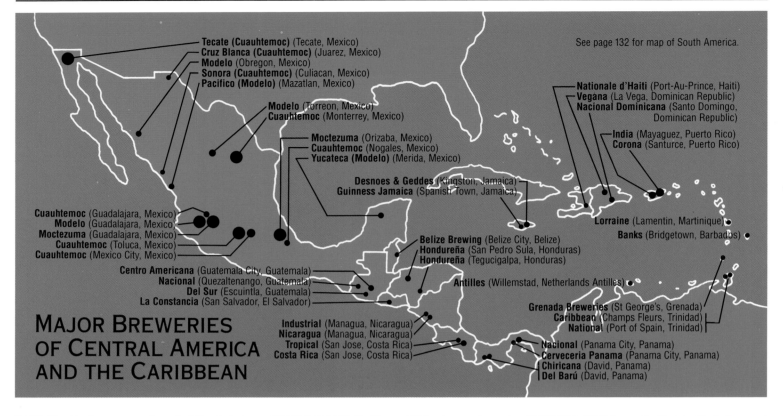

MAJOR BREWERIES OF CENTRAL AMERICA AND THE CARIBBEAN

Tecate (Cuauhtemoc) (Tecate, Mexico)
Cruz Blanca (Cuauhtemoc) (Juarez, Mexico)
Modelo (Obregon, Mexico)
Sonora (Cuauhtemoc) (Culiacan, Mexico)
Pacifico (Modelo) (Mazatlan, Mexico)

Modelo (Torreon, Mexico)
Cuauhtemoc (Monterrey, Mexico)

Moctezuma (Orizaba, Mexico)
Cuauhtemoc (Nogales, Mexico)
Yucateca (Modelo) (Merida, Mexico)

Cuauhtemoc (Guadalajara, Mexico)
Modelo (Guadalajara, Mexico)
Moctezuma (Guadalajara, Mexico)
Cuauhtemoc (Toluca, Mexico)
Cuauhtemoc (Mexico City, Mexico)

Centro Americana (Guatemala City, Guatemala)
Nacional (Quezaltenango, Guatemala)
Del Sur (Escuintla, Guatemala)
La Constancia (San Salvador, El Salvador)

Industrial (Managua, Nicaragua)
Nicaragua (Managua, Nicaragua)
Tropical (San Jose, Costa Rica)
Costa Rica (San Jose, Costa Rica)

Desnoes & Geddes (Kingston, Jamaica)
Guinness Jamaica (Spanish Town, Jamaica)

Belize Brewing (Belize City, Belize)
Hondureña (San Pedro Sula, Honduras)
Hondureña (Tegucigalpa, Honduras)

Antilles (Willemstad, Netherlands Antilles)

Nationale d'Haiti (Port-Au-Prince, Haiti)
Vegana (La Vega, Dominican Republic)
Nacional Dominicana (Santo Domingo, Dominican Republic)

India (Mayaguez, Puerto Rico)
Corona (Santurce, Puerto Rico)

Lorraine (Lamentin, Martinique)
Banks (Bridgetown, Barbados)

Grenada Breweries (St George's, Grenada)
Caribbean (Champs Fleurs, Trinidad)
National (Port of Spain, Trinidad)

Nacional (Panama City, Panama)
Cerveceria Panama (Panama City, Panama)
Chiricana (David, Panama)
Del Barú (David, Panama)

See page 132 for map of South America.

BELOW: The Moctezuma export product line includes Bohemia and Dos Equis as well as Tecate, a formerly independent brand from Baja California, and Sol, a pale 'clara' lager created for American tastes.

FACING PAGE, NEAR: Pacifico and Chihuahua are brewed by breweries which date from 1900 and 1933, respectively. Although both are now part of the Valores portfolio, they retain their brand identification.

FACING PAGE, RIGHT: Brewed by Modelo, Mexico's second largest brewing company, Corona is a pale 'clara' lager that was on the US market for years when clever marketing made it the number two import in 1986.

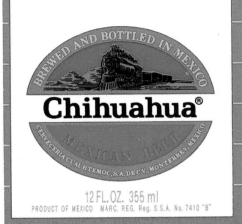

Toluca & Mexico, owned by Agustin Marendes, another Swiss citizen, was established in 1865, and in 1869, Emilio Dercher, an Alsatian, established a small brewery in Mexico City. Lager was first brewed in Toluca, and Don Juan Ohrner in Guadalajara was the second brewer to launch lager on the market.

It was in 1890 that there was established—for the first time in Mexico—a brewery intended as a large enterprise. This was Cervecería Cuauhtémoc, born in Monterrey, which was founded to integrate the delicate art of brewing beer and the technology necessary for large-scale industrial production. This decision resulted in Mexico receiving the first Grand Prize granted for beer at the Chicago International Beer Exposition in 1893.

In 1894, the Cervecería Moctezuma was established by Henry Manthey, William Hasse, C Von Alten and Adolph Burhard in Orizaba, Veracruz. Moctezuma's flagship brands are Dos Equis (XX), which is extremely popular in the United States, and Superior. Other brands include Tres Equis (XXX), Sol, Noche Buena and Bavaria.

In 1890, attorney Francisco Sada, Francisco G Sada and José María Schnaider joined Don José Calderón and their main partners, Isaac Garza and José Mugerza, in order to convert the small annex of Casa Calderón into the Fabrica de Cerveza y Hielo Cuauhtémoc, SA. The latter produced, on a daily basis, two tons of ice and enough beer

to fill 1500 bottles. Soon its brands—Carta Blanca, Saturno, Salvator and Bohemia—were known throughout Mexico. Cervecería Cuauhtémoc, named for the Aztec emperor who died in 1521 and headquartered in Monterrey, Nuevo Leon, was Mexico's second largest brewer prior to its being joined with Moctezuma under the Valores holding company. It is the brewer with the largest number of breweries (seven) in Mexico.

The first beer made by Cervecería Cuauhtémoc was put into a bottle topped with a cap which was fastened on by a wire as with champagne and cider bottles. These first bottles were fitted into heavy, wooden barrels which were later replaced by wooden boxes that could accommodate up to 90 bottles.

The Carta Blanca brand, launched in 1890, was a lager of the pilsener category and became one of the biggest selling beers in Mexico. Bohemia, a dark lager, was launched in 1905. Originally it was bottled in transparent bottles. This practice continued until 1958, when the bottle was changed to a dark one. The Tecate name is derived from 'ish-takat,' or fallen stick, and from a town located in the state of Baja California, where

it was first brewed in 1954. A year later, Cervecería Cuauhtémoc bought the brewery and launched Tecate—a lager beer frequently served, both in Mexico and in the United States, with salt and fresh lemon—in its unmistakable red can. The Chihuahua brand was born in the state of Chihuahua in 1933. Its initial presentation was a transparent amber-hued bottle which was not changed until 1981. Chihuahua is a pale ('clara') lager. The Indio brand goes back to 1905. Initially it was distributed exclusively in the state of Nuevo León, but today it is sold in almost all of the states of Mexico. Bottled in a transparent amber-colored bottle, it was exported to the United States from 1977 to 1981.

Cervecería del Pacifíco of Mazatlán in the state of Sinaloa was established in 1900 by Jacob Schuehle, who had also built the original Moctezuma brewery. The brewery is now owned by Modelo but retains its original brands, Pacifíco Oscura, Pacifíco Clara and Ballena. Pacifíco Oscura is also brewed by Modelo in Guadalajara and Ciudad Obregon.

In 1896, Juan Terrazas founded the Compañía Chihuahua, and in the same year,

Bavaria (Santa Marta, Colombia)
Aguila (Barranquilla, Colombia)
Polar (Maracaibo, Venezuela)
Cervecera Nacional (Barquisimeto, Venezuela)
Polar (Caracas, Venezuela)
Cervecera Nacional (Caracas, Venezuela)
Oriente (Barcelona, Venezuela)
Regional (Maracaibo, Venezuela)
Unión (Caracas, Venezuela)
Banks (Georgetown, Guyana)
Bavaria (Cúcuta, Colombia)
Bavaria (Bucaramanga, Colombia)
Surinaamse Brouwerij (Paramaribo, Suriname)
Unión (Medellin, Colombia)
Andina (Bogotá, Columbia)
Bavaria (Bogotá, Columbia)
Bavaria (Villavicencio, Colombia)
Cacador (Cacador, Brazil)
Paraense (Belém, Brazil)
Maranhense (São Luis, Brazil)
Bavaria (Manizales, Colombia)
Bavaria (Pereira, Colombia)
Bavaria (Neiva, Colombia)
Bavaria (Cali, Colombia)
Bavaria (Pasto, Colombia)
Brahma (Manaus, Brazil)
Antarctica (Manaus, Brazil)
Andina (Quito, Ecuador)
Nacionales (Guayaquil, Ecuador)
Brahma (Fortaleza, Brazil)
Antarctica (Olinda, Brazil)
Cervecera del Norte (Chiclayo, Peru)
Antarctica (Camacari, Brazil)
Cervecera de Trujillo (Trujillo, Peru)
Brahma (Camacari, Brazil)
San Juan (Pucallpa, Peru)
Brahma (Cuiabá, Brazil)
Brahma (Mateus Leme, Brazil)
Anarctica (Goiânia, Brazil)
Brahma (Anápolis, Brazil)
Nacional de Cerveza (Callao, Peru)
Reunidas Skol-Caracu (Brasilia, Brazil)
Antarctica (Pirapora, Brazil)
Cervecera del Sur (Cusco, Peru)
Cervecera del Sur (Arequipa, Peru)
Corumbaense (Corumbá, Brazil)
Antarctica (Belo Horizonte, Brazil)
Kaiser (Belo Horizonte, Brazil)
Nacional Boliviana (La Paz, Bolivia)
Antarctica (Ribeirão Preto, Brazil)
Taquiña (Cochabamba, Bolivia)
Antarctica (Marilia, Brazil)
Weiss (Juiz de Fora, Brazil)
Nacional Santa Cruz (Santa Cruz, Bolivia)
Reunidas Skol-Caracu (Londrina, Brazil)
Kaiser (Nova Iguacu, Brazil)
Brahma (Cabo, Brazil)
Unidas (Antofagasta, Chile)
Antarctica
Brahma
Kaiser
Industrial Cervecera (Salta, Argentina)
Princeza
Cervecerías de Cuyo (San Miguel, Argentina)
Reunidas Skol-Caracu
Paraguaya (Asunción, Paraguay)
Sul Americana
Paraguaya (Caaguazu, Paraguay)
(Rio de Janeiro, Brazil)
Unidas (La Serena, Chile)
Cervecerías de Cuyo (Godoy Cruz, Argentina)
Antarctica (Campinas, Brazil)
Brahma (São Paulo, Brazil)
Cervecera Santiago (Quilicura, Chile)
Antarctica (São Paulo, Brazil)
Paraense (São Paulo, Brazil)
Unidas (Talca, Chile)
Brahma (Curitiba, Brazil)
Antarctica (Joinvile, Brazil)
Unidas (Concepción, Chile)
Antarctica (Ponta Grossa, Brazil)
Brahma (Passo Fundo, Brazil)
Brahma (Porto Alegre, Brazil)
Antarctica (Porto Alegre, Brazil)
Unidas (Osorno, Chile)
Compañia Salus (Salus, Uruguay)
Austral (Puerto Montt, Chile)
Fábricas Nacionales (Montevideo, Uruguay)
Cervecería Paysandú (Paysandú, Uruguay)
Quilmes (Buenos Aires, Argentina)
Bieckert (Buenos Aires, Argentina)
Cervecería Santa Fe (Santa Fe, Argentina)
Cervecería Argentina (San Carlos de Bariloche, Argentina)
Córdoba (Córdoba, Argentina)

MAJOR BREWERIES OF SOUTH AMERICA

See page 130 for map of Central America and the Caribbean.

Jacob Schuehle, George Gruning and Dr Hoeffer founded the Cervecería de Sonora. In 1900, Cervecería del Pacífico was established in Mazatlán, and in Mérida the Cervecería Yucatéca was founded by Jose Maria Ponce y Cia. Like Pacifíco, it is now owned by the Modelo Group, though members of the Ponce family still manage the brewery. Production is divided between Yucatéca's house brands and the parent company's Corona. The Yucatéca brands include Carta Clara, Leon Negra and Montejo.

Cervecería Modelo, headquartered in Mexico City, DF, is Mexico's largest single brewing company. Modelo's annual production is greater than that of all but five American brewers and greater than any of Canada's brewers. Modelo's well-known Corona brand, which has been brewed in Mexico for decades and exported to the United States for years, became a phenomenal 'overnight' success in 1986 in the American market.

Cervecería Cruz Blanca of Juarez, Chihuahua, is the only existing Mexican brewing company founded after 1900. It brews Austriaca, Chihuahua and Liston Azul, in addition to the flagship Cruz Blanca. Belonging to the Cervecería de Sonora, the exquisite High Life beer was launched on the local market in 1923. In 1971, it became part of the Cuauhtémoc group and it is manufactured in the plant at Culiacán in the state of Sinaloa. It is a clear lager.

Brewing in Mexico did not develop as quickly as it did in the United States and Canada, but it has made great strides since the 1970s when Mexico surpassed Canada as North America's second biggest brewing nation. By this time, many of Mexico's brands were available as imports in the United States. Indeed, the largest growth by any imported brands in the American market has been among Mexican beers. In 1986 alone, Moctezuma's Tecate enjoyed a 28 percent increase in popularity, while Modelo's Corona increased its share by an incredible *169 percent*, an unprecedented increase that made it second only to Heineken among imported beers in the United States market.

Like Canada, Mexico's current brewing scene is overwhelmingly dominated by a big three, of which two have merged to leave a big two. Cuauhtémoc, Moctezuma and Modelo all developed from breweries established in the late nineteenth century by German or Swiss immigrants. Cuauhtémoc and Moctezuma joined under the umbrella of Valores Industriales in September 1985, becoming the largest brewing company in Mexico and fifteenth largest in the world. Both partners continue, however, as separate operating groups, and are listed below in their pre-merger configurations. They have separate foreign distribution, but share a common distribution network within Mexico.

Brazil is the second largest brewing nation in the Western Hemisphere, a third again larger than third place Mexico, and with about one-fifth of the production of the United States. The other major South American brewing nations are Columbia and Peru. Chile, a major wine producer, does not rank as one of the hemisphere's leaders. With much of Mexico's production being ex-

TOP: South American lagers include Peru's Cuzco, Columbia's Aguila (Eagle), and Brazil's Brahma, the best-selling beer in Latin America. Xingu is an indigenous 'black beer,' brewed in the pre-Columbian manner. ABOVE: Though not as dark as Xingu, Modelo's Negra is the definitive Mexican dark lager.

ported to the United States, the largest single *brand* of beer sold in all of Latin America is Brahma, which is brewed in Rio de Janeiro, Brazil, by Cervejaria Brahma.

In Central America, the total beer production is less than six million barrels (six million hectoliters), but the area has a long brewing tradition. Today, however, the tradition has shown more direct influence from German-trained brewers in the latter twentieth century than any of the nations to the north. German-style lagers and pilseners are much more common than in Mexico, owing to the region's more tropical climate.

Cervecería Hondureña evolved through mergers with different companies that operated in the early years of the century (1915-1965). These companies individually marketed the Salva Vida (1916) brand in La Ceiba, the Imperial (1930) and Nacional (1953) brands in Teguciagalpa, and the Ulva (1928) brand in San Pedro Sula. The prod-

ucts of the brewery include Imperial, Nacional, Salva Vida and Port Royal Export. The Port Royal and Salva Vida brands were exported to the United States beginning in 1985 and 1988, respectively.

Cervecería Nacional of Panama City was founded in 1909 and is Panama's largest brewer. The company's brands include Atlas, Balboa and Malta Vigor. The company also owns Cervecería Chiricana. Nacional is also the Central American licensee and brewer of Löwenbräu, the famous Munich brand.

The brewing tradition of the little golden flecks which are the islands of the Caribbean is long and varied. In the beginning it was the aboriginal people and their *tesguino* beer and then the English with their imported beers. Some other names given these early brews were *chicha*, *izquiate*, *sendecho*, *zeydetha* and *zeyrecha*. By the seventeenth century, when brewing was really taking hold on the mainland to the north, the isles of the West Indies

had already gone over en masse to the warm embrace of rum.

By the nineteenth century there was the enigmatic Guinness West Indies Porter that may have been brewed there, perhaps in Barbados or possibly Jamaica. It may even have been brewed in the British Isles and brought to the Keys at high tide by wily traders who pretended that it was the local brew. No lager could be brewed there because there was no ice, but then English tastes tended to give lager a wide berth in any event, and it was English tastes that formed the tastes of West Indian beer drinkers. Under license from Dublin, Guinness is today actually brewed in Jamaica.

By 1898, there were just seven breweries in the entire region: one each in Barbados, Trinidad and Cuba, and four in Jamaica. When the United States defeated Spain in the Spanish-American War, Obermeyer & Liebmann came south from Brooklyn to open a

CLOCKWISE FROM ABOVE: These selected Caribbean and Central American beers cover a range of styles and include Bohemia from the Dominican Republic, Banks Jubilee Stout from Barbados, Medalla from Puerto Rico, Pilsener from El Salvador and Desnoes & Geddes' Red Stripe. FACING PAGE: The product line of Cervecería Hondureña.

second brewery in Cuba's capital. Today there are still eight, but the faces of the players have changed. Nacional Dominicana operates two breweries in Santo Domingo, Dominican Republic, which have a total annual capacity of nearly two million barrels (2.4 million hectoliters), and as such, is the largest brewer in the Caribbean.

Desnoes & Geddes of Kingston, Jamaica, was founded in 1918 as a soft drink business by Eugene Desnoes and Thomas Geddes. It is today managed by their heirs, with Peter Desnoes as the most recent past chairman and Paul Geddes as the current chairman. Red Stripe Lager and Dragon Stout are the flagship brands.

Red Stripe was originally ale, but was reformulated as a lager in 1934. Red Stripe is the Caribbean's best known brand elsewhere on the continent.

Holland's giant brewer, Heineken, the largest in Europe, licensed its products to Desnoes & Geddes, but owns breweries in the Antilles and Trinidad.

THE NETHERLANDS

I n medieval times, the present-day Netherlands, like neighboring Belgium, was an important brewing center known for its numerous small village breweries which produced dark, top-fermented beers. Today, although a single brand—Heineken—dominates the Dutch market like no other single brand in any other country on earth, there is a growing resurgence of small, independent brewing companies and brewpubs.

Nevertheless, for many people, that single brand is the emblem of the Dutch beer market. That brand is the flagship brand of Heineken NV. There is probably no brand with the global market penetration of Heineken lager, and the company is in fact the largest brewer on earth, except for the American giant Anheuser-Busch.

The story of Heineken began in 1863, when Gerard Adriaan Heineken noticed that lager beer was becoming more popular than the darker, top-fermented beers brewed by the Netherlands' 559 small brewing companies. There is a an apocryphal tale that Gerhard told his mother of an ambitious proposal in which he would rid Amsterdam's Sunday-morning streets of wayward souls who had enjoyed too much of their home-made brews the night before. Gerard proposed that the way to get people to stop drinking hard liquor was to offer a lighter alternative—of a consistent quality. If she would only provide the money, he could do just that.

Gerard Heineken had his eye on De Hooiberg (The Haystack), an old brewery and well-known Amsterdam establishment dating from 1592. After convincing his mother of the merits of his plan, he bought the building in 1864 and installed the necessary equipment for brewing and cold-fermenting lager. Soon afterward, he built another brewery just outside the city limits, and in 1874 he expanded even further, with the opening of a brewery in Rotterdam.

Whether or not Heineken succeeded in ridding Amsterdam's streets of its drunks is not known, but he quickly became one of his nation's most successful brewers. With a domestic market share and production base firmly in place, the way was paved for exports to France and other European markets. Around the 1920s, Gerard Heineken's son and heir, Henry Pierre Heineken, decided that the key to survival and further growth was expansion into markets outside Europe. This included the Netherlands East Indies (today Indonesia), Africa, the Caribbean and the Far East. On 14 April 1933, soon after the repeal of Prohibition, Heineken became the first European beer imported into the United States.

Today Heineken remains the number one imported beer in the United States and throughout the world. In fact, the Heineken NV company proudly notes that it has exported more beer than has any single country, no matter how many national brands are combined. More than 100 breweries operate under the company's supervision, producing Heineken and a variety of popular national beers all over the world. The production of these beers accounts for sales in roughly 55 of Heineken's 170 foreign

LEFT: An early poster showing the Heineken breweries around the Netherlands. RIGHT: That famous label.

markets. The rest, including the American market, are reached through exports from the Netherlands.

The production at the brewery built by Heineken in Rotterdam has been relocated to larger, more modern facilities in Zoeter-woude, which has a production capacity of nearly six million barrels (seven million hectoliters) per year. The Heineken plant at 's-Hertogenbosch has a capacity of 3.7 million barrels (4.5 million hectoliters). Brewing in smaller quantities continues at the Amsterdam plant, which serves as the showcase brewery.

At the end of the nineteenth century, the largest brewing companies in the Netherlands were Oranjeboom (Orange Tree) in Rotterdam and Amsterdam's Van Vollenhoven, Amstel and Heineken. There was also a good deal of competition in the form of imports from Germany's lager breweries.

In this environment, especially a small country, there was need for cooperation. In March 1900, 10 large breweries in the northern and southern parts of the country established the Bond van Eigenaren en Directeuren van Brouwerijen in Nederland (Union of Owners & Directors of Breweries in the Netherlands). The impending cloud of World War I (1914-1918) convinced the smaller breweries in the southern Netherlands to join forces in the Nederlandsche Bond van Brouwers (Dutch Brewers' Union). A shortage of raw materials resulted in a disastrous decline in beer production in 1917, which forced 150 breweries to close their doors.

On 18 March 1920, De Dreihoek (The Triangle) was established. It was a cooperative agreement between Amstel, Heineken and Oranjeboom, the three largest breweries in the Netherlands. The members of The Triangle agreed not to attempt to expand

MAJOR DUTCH BREWERIES PURCHASED BY HEINEKEN

De Hooiberg (Amsterdam) (1863)
Griffioen (Silvolde) (1919)
Schaepman (Zwolle) (1920)
Rutten (Amsterdam) (1920)
Marres (Maastricht) (1932)
DeKroon (Arnhem) (1934)
Twentsche Stoom Beiersch (Almelo) (1934)
Van Vollenhoven* (Amsterdam) (1941)
St Servatius (Maastricht) (1952)
Vullinghs (Sevenum) (1952)
De Sleutel (Dordrecht) (1953)
Henquet (Eysden) (1959)
Amstel (Amsterdam) (1968)

*Purchased jointly with Amstel

BELOW: A collection of labels from Heineken and brands that became part of Heineken in the latter part of the twentieth century.

Cross-town rivals at the turn of the twentieth century, Heineken and Amstel formed a cooperative agreement in 1920. Oranjeboom was also part of the 1920 pact known as 'The Triangle.'

ABOVE: These posters from the late 1940s celebrate Heineken's quality, and the euphoria of a nation recently delivered from German occupation. It is interesting to note on the bottom poster that three glasses of the still-familiar Heineken Pilsener are accompanied on the tray by a pair of pints of 'oud bruin,' the traditional Dutch brown beer.

LEFT: Heineken's flagship lager (known as Heineken Pilsener at home) is seen here in the uniform that it wears on the export market. These green bottles (and cans) constitute the most widely recognized brand of beer in the world, seen in about 150 nations around the globe. A half billion bottles are exported annually, but Heineken also operates breweries outside the Netherlands to satisfy local demand.

BELOW: The Amstel Brewery was founded in 1870 by CA de Pesters and JH van Warwijk Kooy. Named for the river that winds through the city of Amsterdam, Amstel was second only to Heineken (RIGHT) from the turn of the twentieth century until the two joined forces in 1968.

their clientele at the expense of the other members. During the worldwide depression of the 1930s, competition was regulated by mutual agreement, and the members of the Union of Dutch Breweries maintained a reasonably united stand. The Triangle was disbanded and Amstel and Heineken entered into a 'gentlemen's agreement' in February 1937 to safeguard one another's clientele. This agreement constituted the foundation of the pre-war cooperation between Amstel and Heineken, one of the results of which was the collective acquisition of the Van Vollenhoven Brewery in Amsterdam in 1941. Named for the river that flows through Amsterdam, the Amstel Brewery had been the Netherlands' number two brewer since the beginning of the twentieth century. It was founded in 1870 by CA de Pesters and JH van Warwijk Kooy. As the Dutch market recovered after World War II, Heineken had a 25 percent market share in the Netherlands, compared to 17 percent for Amstel. By the 1960s, the top tier of the Dutch market was divided 31 and 19 percent respectively, although Heineken had a much larger share of the draft beer market in the country and a vastly stronger position overseas. Against this backdrop, Amstel and Heineken began merger talks in 1962, leading them to join forces in 1968, although Amstel continued to operate within the Heineken group from its own Amsterdam brewery and has independent brand identification.

Possibly the best-known Dutch beer after Heineken and Amstel is Grolsch lager. In 1615, Jenneken Neerfelt, daughter of the owner of a local brewery in the town of Grol, married an enterprising young man named Peter Cuyper. An excellent brewer, Cuyper was, in 1677, appointed Guild Master over

ABOVE: Based in Enschede in the eastern Netherlands, Grolsch boasts a thoroughly modern brewing facility. It exists against the backdrop of a tradition dating to 1615, when Peter Cuyper married Jenneken Neerfelt and worked his way into her father's business.

RIGHT: Looming legions of gleaming copper brew kettles at Heineken's brewery in 's-Hertogenbosch.

all the brewers in Grol (now Groenlo). He introduced the brewers to proper techniques and also taught his secrets to succeeding generations. Among the other larger brewing companies in the Netherlands are the likes of Oranjeboom (Orange Tree) in Rotterdam, Brand in Wylre, and Drei Hoefijzers (Three Horseshoes) in Breda.

The Brand Brewery, the oldest brewery in the country, is located in Limburg, the southern-most part of the Netherlands. Records dating from 1340 indicate that a brewery existed in the tiny hamlet of Wylre, which was chosen as a location for a brewery because of the availability of pure, natural spring water. The water passes through layers of chalk, gravel and sand and this filters away the very last of any impurities, making it perfect for brewing. In 1871, Frederik Edmond Brand, urged by his wife's nostalgia for her birthplace, decided to purchase the centuries-old brewery of Wylre. Brand Brewery is today one of the more important breweries in the Netherlands.

Another, smaller brewery is Dommelsche, founded by Willem Snieders at Dommelen in 1744. Dommelsche brews a pils, which is a Pilsen-style lager and Oud Bruin a dark ale, while Bokbier and Dominator are a bock and a doppelbock, respectively.

Located in Maastricht in the province of Limburg at the southern tip of the Netherlands, De Gulpener is a family-owned brewery founded in 1825 by Laurent Smeets, a man who combined the profession of brewer with that of Justice of the Peace. His brewery, called De Gekroonde Leeuw (The Crowned Lion), was maintained by his sons and then in turn by their sons and a son-in-law named Rutten. After three generations, the De Gulpener Brewery passed into the possession of the Rutten family, whose fifth generation now manages the company. Today, Paul Rutten remains true to the principles of craft brewing inherited from his predecessors. As he puts it, 'I blend craft knowledge with technical know-how.'

In addition to brewing a pilsener and an oud bruin (a dark Netherlands beer with a low percentage of alcohol and a high sugar content) Gulpener also produces a number of specialty beers. There is Gulpener Dort, a lightly hopped, Dortmund-style lager, and two seasonal beers: a bock in autumn and Meibock in the spring. Finally there is Sjoes, which the brewery describes as 'a colorful

TOP LEFT: The Dommelsche products include a Pilsener as well as a traditional Dutch 'Oud Bruin.'

LEFT: The capping device used by Grolsch seems like a novelty today, but in the early days of bottled beer two centuries ago, such devices were standard.

ABOVE: The charming facade of Gulpener's brewery is caught in the early morning sun of a crisp Limburg morning. BELOW: The product lines of the two major regional brewers of Limburg in the southern Netherlands include the traditional 'Oud Bruin' (Old Brown) as well as bock. Imperator is a double bock.

The Oranjeboom Bierbrouwerij (Orange Tree Beer Brewery) traces its lineage to 1538, and derives its name not from citrus orchards, but rather from a reference to the Oranje Nassau lineage that began with William the Silent, prince of Orange (1543-1584), who spearheaded the Dutch drive for independence from Spanish rule, which was finally achieved in 1581.

Today, Oranjeboom is the Netherlands' number two brewing company, employing 1000 workers in this well-lit facility in Breda. In addition to brewing under its own name, the company brews Royal Dutch Posthorn, Breda Royal and Three Horses, mainly for export.

melange of two classical beer types, pilsener and oud bruin.'

The distribution of de Gulpener products was once limited to the immediate region, but its beers are now sold throughout the Netherlands, from the Hotel de Werf on the island of Schiermonnikoog that has a 200-year-old taproom, to the village pub in Mesch-Eijsden.

The Alfa Brewery was founded in 1870 by Joseph Meens. Today, it is still entirely family-owned and still produces several traditional styles of beer. Over the generations Alfa Beer has developed a local and national reputation. Alfa's beers are produced from Hallertau hops from Germany and the Czech Republic and water drawn from local stone wells sunk 160 meters into the ground.

In neighboring Belgium, there are several Trappist abbeys that brew a distinct style of dark and fruity ale. In the Netherlands, there is one, the Abbey of Onze Lieve Vrouw van Koningshoeven near Tilburg. The Trappists at Koningshoeven began brewing in 1884 and today their beers are available on the commerical market under the name La Trappe. There are three La Trappe ales: Dubbel with 6.5 percent alcohol; Tripel with 8 percent; and Quadrupel with 10 percent.

Curiously, the Dutch market in the twentieth century has been quite analogous to the

TOP LEFT: The labels of Arcense Brewery in Arcen include references to Jan Primus (Gambrinus), thirteenth-century duke of Brabant and the legendary king of beer. ABOVE AND LEFT: Posters for La Trappe and Alfa (see caption, facing page).

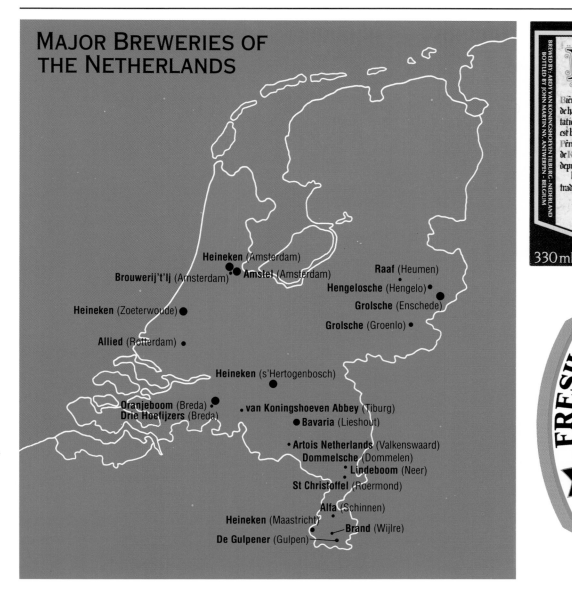

MAJOR BREWERIES OF THE NETHERLANDS

Heineken (Amsterdam)
Brouwerij't Ij (Amsterdam)
Amstel (Amsterdam)
Raaf (Heumen)
Hengelosche (Hengelo)
Heineken (Zoeterwoude)
Grolsche (Enschede)
Grolsche (Groenlo)
Allied (Rotterdam)
Heineken (s'Hertogenbosch)
Oranjeboom (Breda)
Drie Hoefijzers (Breda)
van Koningshoeven Abbey (Tiburg)
Bavaria (Lieshout)
Artois Netherlands (Valkenswaard)
Dommelsche (Dommelen)
Lindeboom (Neer)
St Christoffel (Roermond)
Alfa (Schinnen)
Heineken (Maastricht)
Brand (Wijlre)
De Gulpener (Gulpen)

American market. Troubled times (in the Netherlands, the world wars; in the United States, Prohibition) led to the closing of dozens of small breweries in the first half of the century, while an expanding market in the 1950s and 1960s led to the emergence of powerful national brands, but fewer and fewer actual brewing companies. The number of brewing companies in both countries remained virtually unchanged from the 1960s to the 1980s. Then the idea of small, specialized breweries, which produced unique and very flavorful beers, emerged in the United States as a microbrewery revolution. This phenomena spread to Canada, Britain and ultimately to the Netherlands.

Microbreweries opening in the 1980s included Friesche in Uitwellingerga (1984), Noorder in Alkmaar (1984), Brouwerij 't Ij in Amsterdam (1985) and St Christoffel in Roermond (1986). An older, small brewery, the Arcense in Arcen, was reopened in 1981. One of the most interesting of this new generation of Dutch brewpubs is the brewery and beer museum Raaf (raven), which is situated in the buildings of the former Bergzigt Brewery, which was in the nine-

teenth century the largest in the province of Gelderland. In 1920, Bergzigt closed and the fire under the brew kettle didn't burn for over 60 years. But in 1984, it reopened, having been completely rebuilt. The new facility houses a small-scale brewery, a beer museum and a countryside pub. For the Netherlands, Raaf is a unique museum, featuring among other historic items, the only remaining intact floor malting facility in the country. A video presentation shows the last working floor maltings in the Netherlands in 1952. The museum cinema shows the history of Bergzigt and the restoration of the Raven.

The Raaf Brewery produces beer in the traditional way—without artificial additives—from organically-grown barley malt, hops, yeast and water. Its products include a Pilsen-style lager and beers in the style of Belgian abbey ales and witbiers. A brewery tour, which is part of the museum visit, terminates at the brewery's pub ('proeflokaal,' meaning sampling room) in the former coachhouse of the Bergzigt. There is also an open fireplace, and in summer Raaf opens a terraced beer garden.

ABOVE, FROM TOP: La Trappe has been brewed by the Trappist monks of the Abbey of Onze Lieve Vrouw in Koningshoeven since 1884. The abbey is similar to several Trappist abbeys in neighboring Belgium that are famous for their beer.

Family-owned by the family Meens since 1870, Alfa is one of several independent breweries in Limburg that are active in the export trade.

Also in Limburg is the Bierbrouwerij St Christoffel (Beer Brewery St Christopher), whose beer has been a consistent winner of the Dutch National Taste Test which is held annually over the 'Nederlands Bier Weekend' at the end of June.

Raaf (Raven) is a microbrewery (FACING PAGE, TOP) that opened in 1984 on the site of the Bergzigt Brouwerij in Gelderland. Completely rebuilt, Raaf now houses not only a brewery (FACING PAGE, BOTTOM), but a beer museum as well. Included in the Raaf museum is an early cart (ABOVE) for maneuvering barrels of beer through the narrow streets of Dutch cities. AT RIGHT, unhopped wort makes its way through the grant enroute to the brew kettle. One of Raaf's products is Witte Raaf (White Raven, BELOW), a Belgian-style wheat beer.

UNITED KINGDOM

Brewing in the British Isles has a long and colorful history. Indeed, Samuel Morewood's exhaustive work on the history of Britain noted that 'Watermills were introduced into the country about 500 AD, which enabled the inhabitants to grind their grain and to more easily render it subservient to domestic purposes,' especially the brewing of beer.

Ale was in common use and homemade. Wine was used on some occasions but it was imported. The ancient Britons, at their 'ordinary entertainments, sat down in a ring of rushes, or beds of grass, instead of benches or couches. Three-legged wooden tables were set before them after the manner of the ancient Gauls, covered with victuals, such as bread baked on a gridiron, or under the ashes, milk-meats, flesh and fish both broiled and boiled. The waiters, in the meantime, handed about the drink, in cups made of wood or horn, and sometimes of brass.'

Diodorus Siculus notes in his *History of England* that the love of drink was introduced by the Scots into England. 'The excessive coldness and badness of the climate is the reason that Gaul produces neither grapes nor olives. The Gauls, being destitute of these fruits, make a strong liquor of barley, which they call *zithus*. They also make a kind of drink of honey, diluted with water or wine, which is imported to them by merchants. They are fond of it to distraction, and drink it to excess, until they are either overpowered with sleep or inflamed with a kind of madness. Quarrels often arise among them when they are over their cups, and they start up and fight in the most furious manner, without the least regard to safety or even life.'

Originally the Welsh and Scots had two kinds of ale, called common ale and spiced ale. 'If a farmer hath no mead, he shall pay two casks of spiced ale, or four casks of common ale, for one cask of mead.'

Though sobriety was a virtue among the Normans, by the time of English historian and cleric William of Malmesbury (1090-1143 AD) they had accustomed themselves to the manners of the Britons, and a day and night were spent in feasting without intermission. By a cannon of the Council of Westminster in 1101 AD, however, the clergy were prohibited from frequenting ale houses.

The Anglo-Saxons divided the classes into mild ale, clear ale and Welsh ale, and indeed the Welsh were famous for their ale. Ale, which was then considered to be a national drink, has preserved its reputation to the present time, although it is not so aristocratic as it once was. In earlier times it was served at royal tables. Indeed, the English poet Geoffrey Chaucer (1340-1400) constantly alluded to 'the draught of London ale' and 'the nappy ale of Southwerke.' Another English poet—perhaps the greatest—John

LEFT: At work in a Whitbread brewhouse in Manchester.
FACING PAGE: A perky publican offers a pint of bitter brewed by Stone's, a Bass subsidiary in Yorkshire.

Milton (1608-1674) followed in the footsteps of the father of English poetry in praising the spicy nut-brown ale.

The renowned English satirist Jonathan Swift (1667-1745) was in thorough accord with Archbishop Rolleston when he wrote, 'There is no nation yet known in either hemisphere where the people of all conditions are more in want of some cordial to keep up their spirits than in this of ours.' Bishop Earle showed a true and generous appreciation of the subject when he wrote, 'A tavern is the busy man's recreation, the idle man's business, the melancholy man's sanctuary, the stranger's welcome, the inns-of-courts man's entertainment, the scholar's kindness and the citizen's courtesy.'

The great English lexicographer Dr Samuel Johnson (1709-1784) defined beer as ale brewed with hops to preserve it, 'a liquor made by infusing malt in hot water and then fermenting the liquor' and beer as 'liquor made from malt and hops distinguished from ale, either by being older or smaller.'

ABOVE: Pat and Doug Ord at the bar of their pub, the Chequer Inn in Steyning.

BELOW: Ales being conditioned in oak barrels at Samuel Smith's, the oldest brewery in Yorkshire.

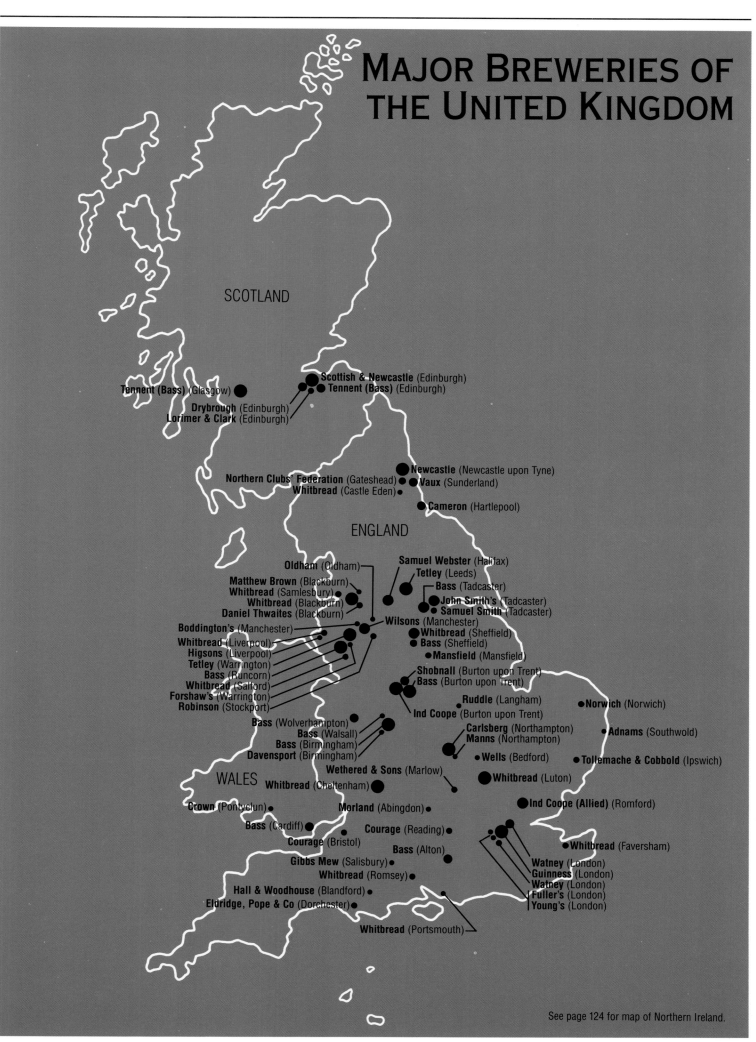

MAJOR BREWERIES OF THE UNITED KINGDOM

SCOTLAND

ENGLAND

WALES

Tennent (Bass) (Glasgow)

Scottish & Newcastle (Edinburgh)
Tennent (Bass) (Edinburgh)
Drybrough (Edinburgh)
Lorimer & Clark (Edinburgh)

Newcastle (Newcastle upon Tyne)
Northern Clubs' Federation (Gateshead) **Vaux** (Sunderland)
Whitbread (Castle Eden)
Cameron (Hartlepool)

Samuel Webster (Halifax)
Oldham (Oldham)
Tetley (Leeds)
Matthew Brown (Blackburn)
Bass (Tadcaster)
Whitbread (Samlesbury)
Whitbread (Blackburn)
John Smith's (Tadcaster)
Daniel Thwaites (Blackburn)
Samuel Smith (Tadcaster)
Wilsons (Manchester)
Boddington's (Manchester)
Whitbread (Sheffield)
Whitbread (Liverpool)
Bass (Sheffield)
Higsons (Liverpool)
Mansfield (Mansfield)
Tetley (Warrington)
Bass (Runcorn)
Shobnall (Burton upon Trent)
Whitbread (Salford)
Bass (Burton upon Trent)
Forshaw's (Warrington)
Robinson (Stockport)
Ruddle (Langham)
Norwich (Norwich)
Ind Coope (Burton upon Trent)
Bass (Wolverhampton)
Carlsberg (Northampton)
Adnams (Southwold)
Bass (Walsall)
Manns (Northampton)
Bass (Birmingham)
Davensport (Birmingham)
Wells (Bedford)
Tollemache & Cobbold (Ipswich)
Wethered & Sons (Marlow)
Whitbread (Cheltenham)
Whitbread (Luton)
Crown (Pontyclun)
Ind Coope (Allied) (Romford)
Morland (Abingdon)
Bass (Cardiff)
Courage (Reading)
Whitbread (Faversham)
Courage (Bristol)
Bass (Alton)
Gibbs Mew (Salisbury)
Watney (London)
Whitbread (Romsey)
Guinness (London)
Watney (London)
Hall & Woodhouse (Blandford)
Fuller's (London)
Eldridge, Pope & Co (Dorchester)
Young's (London)

Whitbread (Portsmouth)

See page 124 for map of Northern Ireland.

Ale is still the characteristic beer, and Britain remains the only major brewing nation in the world where ale is the dominant form of beer being consumed.

Ale is defined as beer which is fermented with top-fermenting yeast (*Saccharomyces cerevisiae*) at a low room temperature. This contrasts with lager, the world's dominant beer type, which is fermented longer with bottom-fermenting yeast (*Saccharomyces carlsbergensis*) at near-freezing temperatures. The two types of beer are typically served at roughly the same temperatures as they are fermented, so to a world used to cold lager, the British have always been considered by their American cousins as being a mite peculiar for their love of 'warm' beer. Today, however, real ale is becoming more and more popular in North America and lager is enjoying an increasing market share in the United Kingdom so old distinctions are blurring. In fact, lager is today the most popular beer in Scotland and Tennent's Lager has been Scotland's top-selling lager since it first appeared. Hugh Tennent, the son of this Glasgow brewing family, introduced lager into Scotland in 1885. He had discovered the light colored beer in Europe and suggested that the family company should begin producing it in Scotland.

BASS AND BURTON

There are over 20 breweries in London, but Burton-Upon-Trent in the English Midlands is the historic center of Britain's brewing industry, due largely to the quality of the water drawn from local artesian wells. The water contains gypsum and is perfect for brewing, a fact that had been observed as early as 1002 AD when the Benedictine Monastery of Saint Modwen was founded. The monks, who brewed their own ale, noted an improvement after they moved to Burton, yet the only thing that had changed was the water they had been using.

The Burton Abbey brewhouse continued its daily output of beer until the early seventeenth century when it was taken over by William Paget, secretary to Henry VIII. By 1600, Burton had 46 inns with attached brewhouses of what would today be called brewpubs. A century later, commercial breweries began to appear on the shores of the River Trent, which had become a major thoroughfare for shipping traffic after passage of the Trent Navigation Act in 1669.

In 1777, William Bass, who ran a cartage business hauling ale to London, opened his own brewery in Burton. He died 10 years later, but his son Michael carried on the business, and by 1800 he had a thriving trade exporting beer to the Baltic countries and Russia, as well as to Danzig and other German states. Bass was on its way to becoming what it is today, Britain's largest brewing company.

In 1806, the scene changed dramatically. Napoleon banned imports of British ale to Europe and the business of all British brewers suffered. It was not until the end of the Napoleonic wars that business picked up

Founded in 1777 at Burton-Upon-Trent by William Bass, Bass & Company is today the largest brewing company in the United Kingdom, and boasts the oldest registered trademark (the red triangle) in the world.

ON THESE PAGES are representative products from Bass, as well as from other brewers that have merged with Bass over the years. Represented by the draft handle at left, Worthington is also a Burton-born brewery.

Brewed at the Cannon Brewery in Yorkshire, Stone's was a popular regional brand until Bass took it national. Brewed by Bass in the UK, Carling Black Label originated with Carling in Canada.

Tennent's was founded in 1885 by Hugh Tennent, the Glasgow brewer who introduced lager to Scotland. Tennent's is now the most popular lager in Scotland.

again. Politically, the defeat of Napoleon at Waterloo in 1815 assured Britain's role as the leading world power. The British Empire, despite that little uprising that flared up in North America in 1776, grew and expanded. India became the crown jewel, and the British soldiers stationed there grew thirsty. In 1832, Bass developed a new top-fermented beer in Burton which was called 'India Pale Ale.' It was so named because it traveled well, even to distant India, as well as to Egypt and South Africa.

India Pale Ale also sold well in the reopened Baltic market, but ironically, Bass never fully exploited the market within Britain—except for London, Liverpool and Burton itself—until the opening of the railway through Burton in 1839, which eventually led to opening up the entire United Kingdom market.

This contributed to the success of Bass and Burton's brewing industry in general. A remarkable expansion took place, and by the Bass centennial in 1877, output had reached a million barrels (1.2 million hectoliters) annually, and the bottles with the little red triangle were being sold on America's Union Pacific Railroad. Meanwhile, across town, Charrington, with whom Bass would ultimately merge, was already brewing 80,000 barrels (95,000 hectoliters).

Ind Coope, now the cornerstone of Allied-Lyons, is second only to Bass among Britain's largest brewing companies. Brewing originally began at the Star Inn in Romford during the mid-eighteenth century when the innkeeper there started brewing beer and his reputation quickly spread. In 1779, Edward Ind purchased this thriving business and John Smith successfully managed it. In 1845, WOE Coope and his brother George bought Smith out, and the brewhouse of the Star Inn became the Romford Brewery, and the firm of Coope & Company was established.

Though the Romford Brewery was successful, the company was attracted to Burton because of the water and the fact that it was clearly the center of the British brewing industry. In 1856, Ind Coope bought a new brewery on Burton's Station Street adjoining the Allsopp Brewery. Soon Ind Coope was brewing its own Burton ales, including an India Pale Ale, which they branded with the Double Diamond symbol. Within a few years, both Ind Coope and Allsopp's became household names, and in 1934 they merged their businesses to form Ind Coope & Allsopp's, joining their premises to form what today is Ind Coope Burton Brewery. The well-known Skol brand was first brewed in 1973, and currently Ind Coope's Burton Brewery exports to over 40 countries, from Russia to the West Indies.

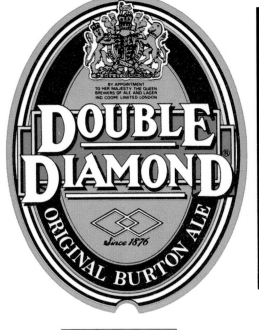

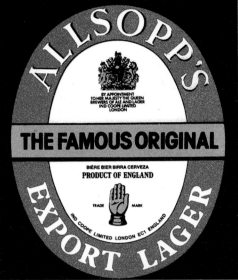

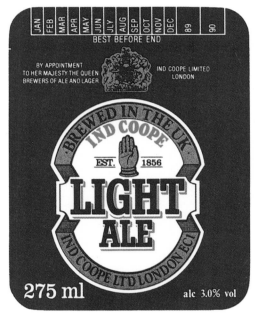

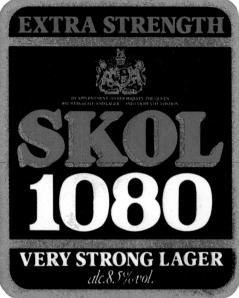

ABOVE: The products of Allied Lyons, the holding company of Ind Coope, the United Kingdom's second largest brewing company. Double Diamond is the Ind Coope flagship brand, while Skol, introduced in 1973, is well-known on the export market.

FACING PAGE, TOP: Noting a growing market for non-alcoholic and low-alcohol beers in the late 1980s, Bass created this portfolio that includes a lager from Tennent's (famous for their lagers) and a bitter ale with the Bass name, as well as an all-new brand.

FACING PAGE, BELOW: The Bass export label is more elegant than the one used in the UK (see previous page).

RIGHT: This selection of products from the Bass portfolio includes former cross-town rival and now subsidiary, Worthington's.

LONDON

The United Kingdom's capital city has a larger number of breweries than any other city in the land, ranging from small brewpubs like the Frog & Furkin and the Orange Brewery in Pimlico Road (which opened in 1983), to large, regional brewing companies like Young's and Fuller's. The three largest British brewers outside Burton—Whitbread, Watney and Courage—are headquartered here, as are Allied-Lyons, the holding company that owns Ind Coope. Guinness of Dublin, Ireland, also maintains a major brewing plant in London to service the British market's need for good Irish stout.

London can also lay claim to being the birthplace of an important beer style. In 1722, a strong, black beer was introduced which used coarse barley and hops that were suited for London's soft water. It is said to have been invented by Ralph Harwood of the Bell Brewhouse. It mainly appealed to market porters, originally those at Covent Gar-

den, who liked both its body and its price. Hence, it became known as 'porter.' The real advantage of porter became clear later when it was made in bulk: It did not deteriorate if matured in wooden casks over a long period of time.

Although the Irish brewers played an important role in the development of porter as a beer style, no one in Britain saw the potential of porter more clearly than Samuel Whitbread. Samuel Whitbread the elder was born on 20 August 1720 in a village near Bedford. At the age of 16, he was apprenticed to work in a brewery in the city of London, which was owned by John Wightman, Master of the Brewers' Company. In 1742, Whitbread formed a partnership and began brewing in London's Whitecross Street. By 1750, he had built a new brewery specifically designed for the mass production of porter, which soon became the staple drink in London. By this time, Whitbread beers were being served in New York.

By 1834, Whitbread's Chiswell Street brewery in London had begun to brew ale, and in 1869, Francis Manning-Needham is credited with having introduced the idea of

bottled beer at Whitbread. By the outbreak of the First World War, more than half of the brewery's output of nearly one million barrels (1.2 million hectoliters) a year was being bottled. Whitbread had become one of the pioneers of packaged beer, along with Worthington and Bass. Brewing finally ceased in Chiswell Street in 1976, and most of Whitbread's beer is now produced at Luton and Malmesbury. Today, Whitbread is the third largest brewing company in Britain after Bass and Ind Coope.

In 1787, John Courage, the Scottish-born son of an exiled French Huguenot family, bought a small brewery in Southwark, London on the south bank of the Thames. Southwark brewing was already renowned, and indeed Chaucer noted its prowess in his fourteenth-century work *Canterbury Tales*. Shakespeare based Falstaff on one of Southwark's leading brewing figures. Pepys viewed the Great Fire of London in 1666 from a Southwark ale house, and Dr Samuel Johnson earned a few quid as an investor in the Thrale family brewery.

Having founded what is today the fifth of Britain's big six, Courage developed valuable

BELOW: The Uxbridge Arms in Notting Hill, London may be Whitbread's oldest pub. BELOW RIGHT: Samuel Whitbread, depicted by Sir Joshua Reynolds in 1787 when he was the leading figure on the London brewery scene.

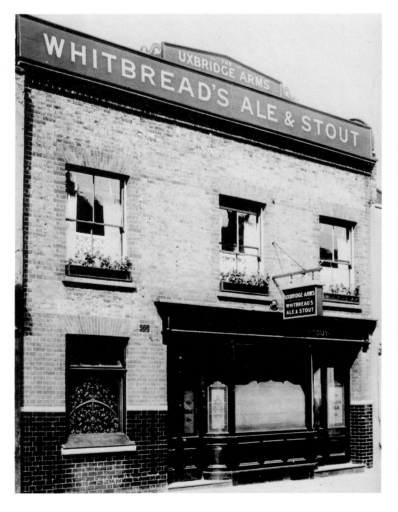

RIGHT: A colonial-era advertisement for John Courage, today the fifth biggest of Britain's brewers.

BELOW: Whitbread's flagship Pale Ale and one of a line of ancillary products which also includes Heineken, brewed for the UK under license from the Netherlands.

BOTTOM ROW: Watney's Cream Stout originated in the seventeenth century, while Red Barrel was designed two centuries later for the export market. London Light is a low-calorie beer developed in the 1980s.

America, take Courage.

John Courage Premium Amber Lager was originally brewed especially for the Royal Navy. It replaced the age-old daily ration of rum.

John Courage is now available and enjoyed throughout the world, wherever tradition and good taste are honoured. A pint will tell you why.

Imported by Century Importers, Baltimore, MD

Call for a JC

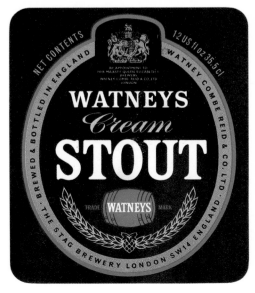

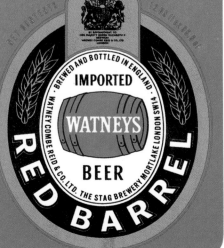

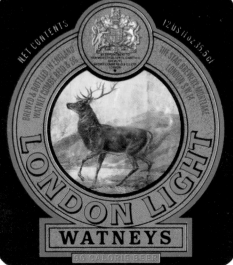

international commerce from his site on the Thames. Trade with the Royal Navy led to the spread of the Courage name throughout the English-speaking world. Interestingly, the origins of John Courage Amber Lager go back in years to a specially developed export beer that rapidly became the Navy's own brand. In fact, it eventually replaced the seaman's daily tot of rum when the Royal Navy ended that long-standing tradition. Today, however, Courage is part of Elders IXL, the Australian group best known as the world-wide distributor of Foster's Lager.

Young & Company's Ram Brewery evolved from a brewery that existed on the River Wandle at Wandsworth (London) in 1675. Charles Allen Young bought the Ram Brewery in 1831. Today Young's—still a Young family business—owns over 150 tied houses, mostly in and around London, and brews a variety of beers for bottling. These have won numerous awards, both from the industry and from the Campaign for Real Ale (CAMRA).

RIGHT: Young & Company's Ram Brewery is highly regarded as one of London's independent 'home town' breweries. Old Nick is one of Britain's most highly-regarded barley wines.

BREWING AROUND BRITAIN

Since 1641, there had been references to the fine beers of Southwold at Sole Bay. The brewery appears to have evolved from the old brewhouse behind the Swan Hotel, the most important inn in Southwold. The name Adnams first appeared in 1872 when the Adnams family arrived from Berkshire to take over the Sole Bay Brewery. A great many medals, cups and awards have been won over the years, pride of place going to the Championship Cup for the Best Beer in Britain, awarded for Champion Pale Ale at the National Brewers' Exhibition, Wine Merchant of the Year in 1991, and First Prize Standard Bitter, awarded at the Great British Beer Festival in 1990.

Established in 1711, Morland is England's second oldest independent brewer, with over 200 pubs, mostly in the Thames Valley region. The Morland 'sign of the artist' dates back to the eighteenth century when George Morland, a relative of the brewing Morlands and one of the region's more well-known painters of that era, was a frequent guest at Morland hostelries. It was in tribute to him that the family chose the artist as their sym-bol. Pallet in one hand, pint in the other, the Morland logo honors both the painter's and the brewer's art.

Founded in 1758 by his family, Samuel Smith's Old Brewery at Tadcaster is the oldest brewery in Yorkshire. Both Dr Samuel Johnson and Oliver Goldsmith frequented Samuel Smith's Tadcaster pubs, and Charles Dickens describes the brewery in his *A Tale of Two Cities*. Today, The beers of Samuel Smith's Old Brewery in Tadcaster include the extraordinary Taddy Porter, Nut Brown Ale, Imperial Stout (reminiscent of the beers brewed in England during the eighteenth century for the Baltic market) and Oatmeal Stout.

Charles Hall founded the Ansty Brewery in 1777. With England at war against France, a large military encampment was set up at Weymouth to counter the threat of invasion. The young brewer quickly secured a government contract for the supply of Ansty Beer to the camp. After the purchase of other local breweries and their houses at the turn of the century, Ansty became a limited company and moved into a new brewery at Blandford St Mary, the company's present headquarters, built at a cost of £28,000. The brothers George Edward and Alfred Woodhouse were the two directors, joined by their youngest brother Frank, who died while serving as chairman in 1952. Since Charles Hall founded the brewery, Hall & Woodhouse has won many national brewing awards for their excellent beers. Badger Best Bitter, a traditional beer dispensed mostly by hand pumps, is now sold in Devon, Hampshire, Berkshire, Surrey, Middlesex, Sussex and Avon, as well as Dorset, Somerset and Wiltshire.

In 1876, Charles Wells retired from his first career as an officer with the Blackwall Frigate Company, for whom he sailed ships around the world to Australia, and bought a small, existing business at Horne Lane in the center of Bedford. Following his death in 1914, his sons continued to develop the business by taking over other brewing companies in and around Bedford, by acquiring more public houses, and by continuing the policy of developing existing pubs. A new brewery at the edge of Bedford was com-

ADNAMS

ORIGINAL GRAVITY 1071–1079°

275 ml

BREWED & BOTTLED AT SOLE BAY BREWERY · SOUTHWOLD · SUFFOLK

"BEST BEFORE END DATE: SEE LABEL EDGE"

TALLY-HO
BARLEY WINE

ADNAMS

ORIGINAL GRAVITY 1032–1036°

275 ml

BREWED BY ADNAMS, SOLE BAY BREWERY · SOUTHWOLD · SUFFOLK

"BEST BEFORE END DATE: SEE LABEL EDGE"

NUT BROWN
ALE

ADNAMS

ORIGINAL GRAVITY 1064–1072°

275 ml

BREWED BY ADNAMS, SOLE BAY BREWERY · SOUTHWOLD · SUFFOLK

"BEST BEFORE END DATE: SEE LABEL EDGE"

1672 BATTLE OF SOLE BAY

BROADSIDE
STRONG PALE ALE

INDEPENDENT FAMILY BREWERS

ESTABLISHED IN THE YEAR 1845

FULLER'S

ESB
ENGLISH ALE

12 Fl. oz. 35.5 cl

Brewed & Bottled by
FULLER SMITH & TURNER PLC · CHISWICK · LONDON · ENGLAND

INDEPENDENT FAMILY BREWERS

ESTABLISHED IN THE YEAR 1845

FULLER'S

LONDON PRIDE
Traditional
ENGLISH BEER

12 Fl. oz. 35.5 cl

BREWED AND BOTTLED BY
FULLER SMITH & TURNER PLC · CHISWICK · LONDON · ENGLAND

TOP AND RIGHT: The Adnams family purchased the Sole Bay Brewery in 1872, which had evolved from a brew-house associated with the Swan Hotel overlooking Sole Bay. Adnams ales are consistent prize winners.

ABOVE: Like Young's, Fuller's is one of London's prominent independent brewers.

ABOVE: Tanglefoot is regarded as one of the best ales in England's West Country. In 1777, the same year that William Bass started brewing in Burton, Charles Hall founded his Ansty Brewery in Weymouth. His son, Robert, invited George Woodhouse into the firm in 1847, and later George married one of Robert's daughters.

LEFT: The mash tun and brew kettle on the floor at Hall & Woodhouse have produced countless batches of beers, under the brewer's watchful eye.

BELOW: The badger became the mascot of the Hall & Woodhouse brewery and is now the company logo. Locals speak of having been 'weaned' on Badger beers.

ABOVE AND FACING PAGE: Samuel Smith's of Tadcaster is Yorkshire's oldest brewery. LEFT: Established in 1711, Morland's of Abingdon, is the model of a successful independent regional brewing company.

pleted in 1976. In turn, penetration of the take-home trade increased dramatically after the first canning line was installed in 1978, and capacity was further doubled by 1992.

Vaux and Sons was founded in 1837 by Cuthbert Vaux at a brewery on the corner of Matlock and Cumberland streets in Sunderland. A half century later, the firm was one of the first to face the demand that was to come for bottled ales and stouts, and Vaux initiated the bottled ale and stout trade in Sunderland. In 1927, Sir Frank Nicholson arranged the merger of C Vaux and Sons, Ltd and the North Eastern Breweries, Ltd, which became Associated Breweries. In 1940, the name was changed to Vaux and Associated Breweries, Ltd, and in 1973 to Vaux Breweries, Ltd. By the 1990s, Vaux had 200 tied houses.

The Gibbs family are believed to have been brewers since the middle of the eighteenth century. The current chairman's great-great-grandfather, John Gibbs (1785-1864), like his father, is known to have brewed at The Swan, Haslemere. John's brother, George Bridger Gibbs, entered a partnership in 1838 with Sydney Fawcett to brew in Endless Street, Salisbury. Gibbs Mew was formed in 1898 to take over the businesses of Messrs Bridger Gibbs & Sons and Herbert Mew & Co, both of Salisbury. The company continues using the exclusive water from its own well, the deepest in the district, drawn from strata different from those used by existing town mains. Today Gibbs Mew supplies 120 of its own public

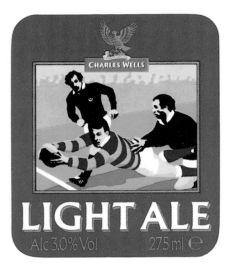

ABOVE: Vaux & Sons of Sunderland also owns Lorimer & Clark of Edinburgh. FACING PAGE, TOP: Named for a retired sea captain who took up brewing in 1876, Charles Wells is based in Bedford. FACING PAGE AND RIGHT: Gibbs Mew's Bishop's Tipple celebrates George Reindorp's becoming Bishop of Salisbury, while Chudley celebrates the commuter railway.

houses and has a substantial free trade business with hundreds of outlets throughout the south and west of England. Gibbs Mew boasts a string of prizes for its brews, such as the Brewing Industry's Gold Medal for its Moonraker Brown Ale.

As in any country, a sizable proportion of British beer sales takes place in taverns and pubs. In Britain, unlike elsewhere, however, most pubs are 'tied houses,' meaning they are 'tied' to a specific brewery and its beers. This makes for a good supply of fresh beer, but it can also be perceived by some as being monopolistic. Thus, in 1986, the UK Monopolies and Mergers Commission began an investigation into the supply of beer in the United Kingdom. Its conclusions became law and required two major changes. From

May 1990, tenants in tied houses could buy one 'guest' ale, and by November 1992, all brewers owning more than 2000 tied pubs had to sell, or lease free of the tie, half of their pubs above this limit. In the case of Bass and Whitbread, for example, the new law meant they each had to sell, or 'free,' more than 2000 pubs.

Perhaps the most important single event in the history of brewing and beer drinking in the past half century in Britain has been the Campaign for Real Ale (CAMRA). From its beginnings in Manchester in 1972, CAMRA was a movement aimed at preventing the takeover of small, regional, traditional ale brewers by huge brewing companies. 'Real ale' in CAMRA's definition is cask-conditioned beer in which fermenta-

tion continues to take place in the wooden barrel from which the beer is served. This contrasts with most draft (in Britain, draught) beers, which are filtered and pasturized before they are put into barrels or kegs.

While CAMRA was not entirely successful in its first objective, it did attract many members and focused a great deal of attention on the decline of traditional ale brewing in Britain. Many such brewers did close their doors, but others thrived. Noted British beer commentator Michael Jackson credits CAMRA with saving cask-conditioned ale as a beer style. CAMRA also influenced the practices of the brewing giants and paved the way for the whole new generation of brewpubs that arrived on the scene in the 1980s and 1990s.

THE UNITED STATES

Today the United States is the world's biggest brewing nation, with an annual output of over 180 million barrels (214 million hectoliters), double that of second-place Germany and triple that of third-place Great Britain. The history of brewing in the United States began with the Indians of Mexico and the American Southwest, but most of our present traditions arrived with the European immigrants. The English brought their top-fermenting ale yeasts with them and immediately established breweries in the Colonies. By the time of the American Revolution, ales and porters were well developed as part of daily life, and most landowners were as likely to have a brewhouse on their grounds as a stable. Among America's early statesmen, not only Samuel

Adams, but both George Washington and Thomas Jefferson were brewers. Next, in 1840, the first wave of German immigrants introduced bottom-fermenting yeasts to American brewing, and the United States soon became a land of lager drinkers.

By the end of the nineteenth century there were 4000 breweries located in nearly every small town and city neighborhood, each with its own special style of beer. The idea of a town or neighborhood brewer was no more unusual than a town baker or neighborhood butcher. The advent of a continental railroad network and the invention of artificial ice made possible the rise of megabrewers like

BELOW: A modern brewpub in San Diego. OPPOSITE: The products of California's Sierra Nevada.

Schlitz, Pabst and Anheuser-Busch, who became large, regional brewers, and by World War II were in a position to launch truly national brands.

With the rise of the national brands, small local and regional brewers suffered, and many disappeared as nearly everyone attempted to create pale lagers that would appeal to as wide an audience as possible. The big American beermakers are all essentially lager brewers. The largest American brewing companies by market share are Anheuser-Busch (with over 40 percent), Miller and Coors. The leading brands by market share are Anheuser-Busch's Budweiser (with over 25 percent), Miller's Lite, Anheuser-Busch's Bud (Budweiser) Light and Coors Light.

Based in St Louis, Anheuser-Busch is not only the largest brewer in the United States, but the largest brewer in the world, with no close rivals. The company traces its roots to a small brewery started in St Louis, Missouri, in 1852 by George Schneider and taken over in 1860 by Eberhard Anheuser. Four years later Anheuser's son-in-law Adolphus Busch joined the firm. A far-sighted marketing genius, Busch turned the small city brewery into a national giant.

Busch launched the extraordinarily successful Budweiser brand as a mass-market beer in 1876, and in 1896 he introduced the still-popular Michelob brand as the company's premium beer. Originally a draft beer, Michelob was not marketed as a bottled beer until 1961. Today Anheuser-Busch's flagship brewery is still located in St Louis, but beginning in 1951 other breweries were established at Newark, New Jersey (1951); Los Angeles, California (1954); Tampa, Florida

LEFT: From its flagship brewery in St Louis, Anheuser-Busch became the world's largest brewing company. ABOVE: The company's product portfolio includes Budweiser, America's biggest-selling brand.

(1959); Houston, Texas (1966); Columbus, Ohio (1968); Jacksonville, Florida (1969); Merrimack, New Hampshire (1970); Williamsburg, Virginia (1972); Fairfield, California (1976); Baldwinsville, New York (1980); Fort Collins, Colorado (1988); and Cartersville, Georgia (1992).

In addition to 'Bud' and Michelob, Anheuser-Busch brews a variety of other beers. Busch, introduced in 1955, is marketed regionally. In 1988 and 1989, Busch received gold medals in the American pilsner category at the Great American Beer Festival. In the late 1970s and early 1980s, the company introduced a family of low-calorie or 'light' beers. These included Natural Light (1977), Michelob Light (1978) and Bud Light (1982). In 1981, Anheuser-Busch introduced Michelob Classic Dark, which has been a consistent award winner at such events as the Great American Beer Festival, where it competes alongside some of the

nation's best specialty beers. In 1984, the company not only added a high-alcohol malt liquor called King Cobra to its family of products, but also became the first major brewer to mass market a reduced-alcohol beer, which they call 'LA.' Anheuser-Busch also introduced a non-alcoholic beer known as O'Doul's in 1990.

In the late 1980s, 'dry' beer became an important phenomenon on the American market. Developed in Europe, dry beer is a lager in which all fermentable sugars have been turned to alcohol, although the final alcohol content is roughly the same as average lager. Introduced in 1988, Anheuser-Busch's Michelob Dry was the first American dry beer, and it was followed by Bud Dry in 1990.

Miller Brewing of Milwaukee has been the second largest brewing company in the United States since the late 1970s after a long climb from eleventh place in 1965. The

brewery originated in suburban Milwaukee, Wisconsin, in 1855 as Charles Best's Plank Road Brewery. It was purchased in 1855 by Frederic Miller, who turned it into one of the region's leading breweries. In 1969 the Philip Morris Tobacco Company acquired 53 percent of Miller Brewing, and the following year they bought the remaining 47 percent. Miller produces over 40 million barrels (48 million hectoliters) annually and operates six plants located at Albany, Georgia; Eden, North Carolina; Irwindale, California; Fort Worth, Texas; Fulton, New York; and Milwaukee, Wisconsin. The Milwaukee brewery is the largest.

For many years, Miller's flagship brand was Miller High Life, a national brand lager that has existed since before Prohibition, and which is still a key part of the Miller product line. However, it has been eclipsed by Miller Genuine Draft, also a pale lager, which was introduced in 1986 and which has

SOME EASTERN REGIONAL BREWERS

Catamount Brewing of White River Junction, Vermont, which produced its first beer in 1987, was the first commercial brewery to operate in Vermont since 1893. Initial distribution included only Vermont and New Hampshire, but has been expanded to other New England states since 1988.

Commonwealth Brewing is located in Boston, Massachusetts.

Dock Street Brewing was founded in 1986 by Philadelphia chef Jeffrey Ware.

DL Geary Brewing was founded in 1988 in Portland, Maine. Brewing of Geary's Pale Ale is under the direction of brewmaster David Geary.

General Brewing Company of Rochester, New York, is the seventh largest brewer in the United States. The company traces it heritage back to the brewery established in 1855 by Jacob Rau. This business evolved into the Genesee Brewing Company in 1878. In February 1985, Genesee bought the Fred Koch Brewery of Dunkirk, New York.

Jones Brewing of Smithton, Pennsylvania, was established by Welsh immigrant William B 'Stoney' Jones in 1907 as the Eureka Brewing Company. The brewery's original brand was Eureka Gold Crown, but because Stoney Jones habitually made personal sales calls to taverns in the area, it came to be known unofficially as 'Stoney's Beer.' The brewery lost little time changing the official name. Until recently, the brewery was operated under the presidency of William B 'Bill' Jones III.

Latrobe Brewing of Latrobe, Pennsylvania, was established in 1893 at a time when the town's only other brewery was located at St Vincent's Abbey and operated by Benedictine monks. The brewery at St Vincent's closed in 1898 after 42 years of operation, but the brewery that took the name of the town survives to this day. The flagship Rolling Rock brand is named for the nearby Rolling Rock Estate, a horse ranch. An intriguing detail about Rolling Rock is the presence of the mysterious '33' symbol that appears on the back of the bottle. The company itself cannot remember why it was put there in the first place because the product was introduced in 1939. However, among the most popular answers to the riddle are that Prohibition was repealed in 1933; there are 33 words on the back of the 12-ounce Rolling Rock bottle; or that there are 33 letters in the ingredients of Rolling Rock—water, malt, rice, corn, hops, brewer's yeast.

The Lion Incorporated of Wilkes-Barre, Pennsylvania, also known as Gibbons Brewery, was founded in 1905 as the Luzerne County Brewing Company and became Lion Brewing in 1910. It was reconstituted as The Lion Incorporated after Prohibition, and has used the Gibbons, Stegmaier and Pocono brand names ever since.

Massachusetts Bay Brewing, a microbrewery which calls itself simply Mass Bay Brewing, is located in Boston, Massachusetts, with distribution throughout New England.

FX Matt Brewing of Utica, New York, (also known as West End Brewing) evolved from the Columbia Brewery established by Charles Bierbauer in 1853. The company was taken over in 1888 by Francis Xavier Matt I (grandfather of the current president, FX Matt II) and organized as West End Brewing. The brewery was renamed for FX Matt in 1980, 22 years after his death. The brand name Utica Club, which was introduced for the soft drinks produced by the company during Prohibition, became so popular that it was retained afterward for West End's beer products.

Olde Heurich Brewing was founded in 1986 in Washington, DC, by Gary Heurich, the grandson of Christian Heurich, who started a brewery in 1873 that overlooked the Potomac on the site now occupied by the Kennedy Center. Christian Heurich supervised the brewery until his death in 1945 at the age of 102. His son kept the brewery in business until 1965.

Founded in Boston by amateur brewer Rick Dugas, Olde Time Brewers began brewing its popular Ironside Ale in 1992.

Yuengling & Son was established in 1829 by David G Yuengling. It stands as the oldest brewery in the United States and, after Molson in Canada (1786), as the second oldest in North America. Today the 200,000-barrel (238,000-hectoliter) brewery is still family owned and operated under president Richard Yuengling.

SOME MIDWESTERN REGIONAL BREWERS

The Berghoff is an old Chicago restaurant famous for its 100-foot bar and for its private label Berghoff Beer, which is regarded by many as Chicago's 'hometown beer.' It traces its heritage to the brewery started in 1887 in Fort Wayne, Indiana, by Herman Josef Berghoff of Dortmund, Germany. Berghoff introduced his beer to the Windy City at the 1893 Chicago World's Fair and opened the restaurant at its present site in 1898. In 1989, Berghoff bought Huber, forming the Berghoff-Huber Brewing Company.

Capital Brewery is a microbrewery opened in June 1986 in the town of Middleton, Wisconsin.

Cold Spring Brewing of Cold Spring, Minnesota, dates back to the brewery started by George Sargel in 1874 and evolved to its present name by 1898.

Dubuque Star Brewing in Dubuque, Iowa, was established as Star Brewing in 1898 and took the name of its hometown in 1904.

Joseph Huber Brewing of Monroe, Wisconsin, evolved from the Bissinger Brewery established in 1845. Between 1848 and 1906, it operated successively under the names John Knipschilt, Ed Ruegger, Jacob Hefty, Fred Hefty and Adam Blumer. It survived as Blumer Brewing until 1947, when it became Joseph Huber Brewing. In 1985, when Paul Kalmanovitz took over Pabst, the latter's president and vice president purchased Huber. In 1989, Huber Brewing was in turn purchased by the Berghoff in Chicago, a restaurant for whom it had long brewed a house brand beer. The resulting company is now known officially as Berghoff-Huber Brewing.

Hudepohl-Schoenling of Cincinnati, Ohio, known locally as 'Cincinnati's Brewery,' was created in December 1986 by the merger of Hudepohl Brewing and Schoenling Brewing. Hudepohl originated with Gottfried Koehler in 1852 and was taken over as the Buckeye Brewery of Ludwig 'Louis' Hudepohl and George Kotte in 1885. The company became Hudepohl Brewing in 1899. In 1982, the company introduced Chris-

tian Moerlein, a brand named for one of Cincinnati's first great brewers, whose famous brewery was started on Elm Street in 1853 but did not survive Prohibition. Schoenling Brewing was established in 1934 on the heels of the repeal of Prohibition.

Kalamazoo Brewing (aka Bell's) is a microbrewery in Kalamazoo, Michigan, with brewing under the direction of Larry Bell.

Millstream Brewing of Amana, Iowa, was founded by Joe Pickett, Sr, with the first bottling in December 1985.

The Oldenberg Brewery of Fort Mitchell, Kentucky, near Cincinnati, is complemented by the Brewery and Entertainment Complex that includes a vast beer hall, beer garden and a restaurant. With the Western Hemipshere's largest collection of brewing memorabilia, Oldenberg is also home to the American Museum of Brewing History & Arts.

August Schell Brewing of New Ulm, Minnesota, was established in 1860. The brewery survived the 1862 Sioux uprising because of August Schell's good relations with the Indians, and has existed as a small regional brewery ever since.

Sprecher Brewing is a microbrewery located in Milwaukee, Wisconsin, with brewing under the direction of master brewer Randy Sprecher.

Stevens Point Brewery of Stevens Point, Wisconsin, dates from the brewery established prior to 1857 by Frank Wahle and George Ruder. By 1902, the brewery had taken its present name. The success of the Stevens Point Brewery and its Point Special Beer was traditionally seen as being due, at least in part, to its decision to limit distribution to a very narrow geographical area, permitting demand to exceed supply.

Summit Brewing is a microbrewery located in St Paul, Minnesota. The principal brands brewed here are Extra Pale Ale, the award-winning Great Northern Porter, Summit Sparkling Ale and Christmas Ale.

CLOCKWISE FROM ABOVE: Miller Brewing's Amber Ale, introduced in 1993; a vintage Miller poster; Miller Genuine Draft, a lager introduced in 1986.

outsold High Life since 1991. Today, the biggest-selling Miller product is Lite, which was introduced in 1975 as the first nationally-marketed, reduced-calorie beer. Lite went on to become the leading reduced-calorie beer, as well as the second best selling beer of any kind in the United States after Budweiser. An important Miller product since 1975 is Löwenbräu, produced under license from the brewer of the same name in Munich, West Germany, where it has been produced since 1893. (In Canada, Molson brews Löwenbräu.) While Miller brews a German beer in the United States, Miller High Life is brewed in Canada by Carling O'Keefe and in Japan by Sapporo.

In March 1993, Miller became the first major American brewing company to introduce and nationally market a full-flavored top-fermented beer in several decades. Called Miller Reserve Amber Ale, the new beer was brewed with 100 percent barley malt and true ale yeast. The result was a distinctive beer more like the specialty beers of the microbrewers' than like what one would expect from a major mass market brewing company. Miller had previously introduced two lagers under the Miller Reserve 'family' which were brewed with 100 percent barley malt. This is in contrast with most American mass-market lagers that use less expensive grains such as rice and cracked corn as adjuncts to the barley. In 1987, Miller acquired Jacob Leinenkugel Brewing of Chippewa Falls, Wisconsin, which was built in 1867 by its namesake and John Miller (no relation), who was Leinenkugel's partner for the next 16 years. Located on top of Big Eddy Springs, the

brewery was known as the Spring Brewery until 1898. After the 1987 acquisition by Miller Brewing, Leinenkugel remained autonomous as a separate operating unit. Every Leinenkugel's label still carries the distinctive Indian maiden head ('Leinie') motif. This reflects the brewery's location in 'Indian Head Country,' so named because of the Indian profile created on maps by the meanderings of the Mississippi River along the Wisconsin-Minnesota border near Chippewa Falls. In the early 1990s, Leinenkugel introduced a variety of specialty beers including Genuine Bock and Red Lager.

In 1993, the two largest brewing companies in Canada (Molson and Labatt) and the United States (Anheuser-Busch and Miller) began to market 'ice' beer. Developed and patented by Labatt in Canada, ice beer is a pale lager which is quickly chilled to subfreezing temperatures after brewing but before final fermentation. The result is the formation of ice crystals in the beer, which are removed to produce a beer with as much as *twice* the alcohol content of typical mass market lagers.

LEFT: The Coors flagship lager. BELOW: The Coors brewery in Golden, Colorado, once the world's largest.

The Adolph Coors Company of Golden, Colorado, operated for 114 years at the same site high in the Rocky Mountains that was selected by Adolph Coors himself in 1873. Coors has grown from one of scores of tiny, regional breweries that once dotted the nation's landscape, to the third largest brewing company in the United States. At the same time, its brewing plant in Golden is the single largest brewery in the world. In 1987, Coors celebrated the grand opening of its second brewery in Virginia's Shenandoah Valley, near the town of Elkton.

The Coors product line is headed by the flagship Coors Banquet brand, the complementary low-calorie Coors Light (which is known as the 'Silver Bullet' because of the natural aluminum finish of its can), and a seasonal beer called Winterfest. Other products include the distinctively colored George Killian's Irish Red, an ale brewed under license from the original Irish brewer.

Stroh Brewery of Detroit became the fourth largest brewing company in the United States in May 1982 when it purchased the much larger, but financially ailing, Joseph Schlitz Brewing Company. Schlitz, whose brand name Stroh retained, had been one of the two largest brewers in the United States since the nineteenth century. Founded in Milwaukee, Wisconsin, a leading lager-brewing city, by August Krug in 1849, the company was taken over by his son-in-law Joseph Schlitz in 1858. Although Schlitz died a year later while boating in his native Germany, the company grew and it's product became known as 'the beer that made Milwaukee famous.'

Started in 1850 by Bernhard Stroh, the company survived Prohibition but remained a regional brewery until well after World War II. The acquisition of Schaefer in 1981 and of Schlitz the following year catapulted Stroh from seventh to fourth place among United States brewers, but Stroh's market share declined through most of the mid-1980s.

Established in La Crosse, Wisconsin, by Gottlieb Heileman and John Gund in 1858, the G Heileman Brewing Company remained a small regional brewer until the early 1960s, when it began to acquire other

BELOW: Stroh now owns Schlitz and Schaefer, while the Heileman portfolio includes many important regionals such as Lone Star of Texas, Blatz of Milwaukee, Rainier of Seattle and Blitz Weinhard of Portland, Oregon.

smaller regional breweries, such as the acquisition of Associated Breweries in 1963 and Blatz in 1969.

Heileman is a unique example of a small regional brewer that grew to national prominence, not through the vehicle of a single national brand like Anheuser-Busch or Miller, but through an amazing amalgam of important, formerly independent, regional brands. Among the major regional brands acquired by Heileman are Oregon's Blitz, Henry Weinhard, Washington's Rainier, Minnesota's Grain Belt and Lone Star, the so-called 'national beer of Texas.' The original Pabst Brewing Company of Milwaukee, Wisconsin, was started in 1844 by Jacob Best and later run by Philip Best in partnership with Captain Frederick Pabst, but the Captain essentially ran the brewery himself after Philip retired in 1866. Pabst was the largest brewery in the United States at the turn of the century and has remained in the top six ever since. Pabst acquired Olympia Brewing in 1983 (which had recently acquired Theodore Hamm's brewery in St Paul, Minnesota).

The major Pabst brand is Pabst Blue Ribbon, one of the oldest name brands in American history. Other Pabst-owned brands

BELOW: Pabst now includes such important regionals as Falstaff; Olympia of Olympia, Washington; and Hamm's from 'the land of sky-blue waters,' St Paul, Minnesota.

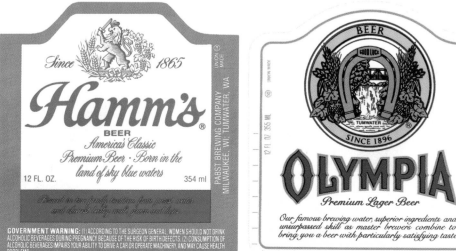

See page 184 for map of the Pacific Coast.

Coors (Golden, CO)

MAJOR BREWERIES OF THE UNITED STATES
(EXCLUDING THE PACIFIC COAST)

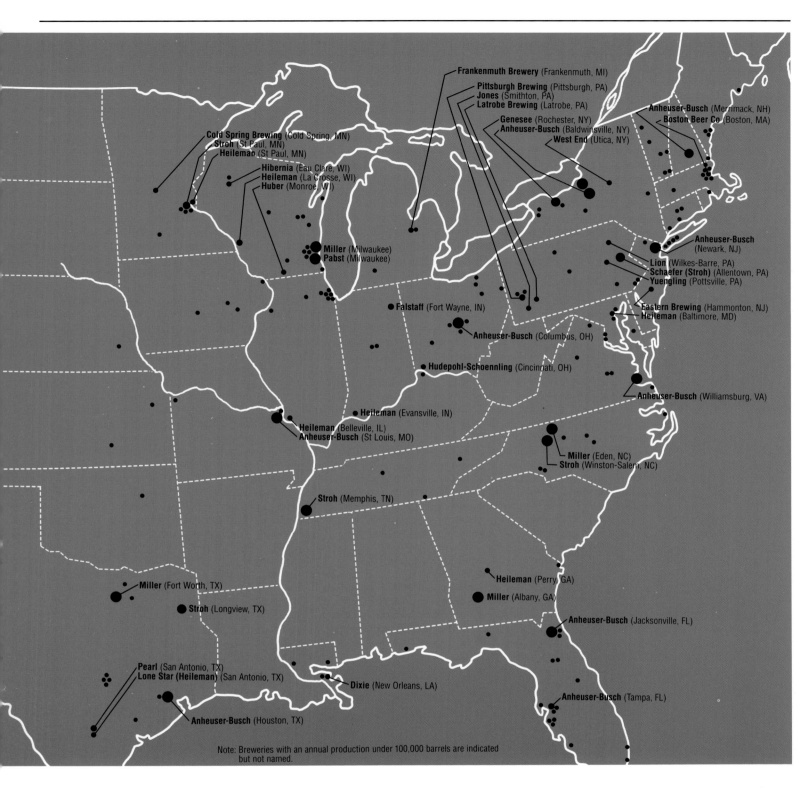

Frankenmuth Brewery (Frankenmuth, MI)
Pittsburgh Brewing (Pittsburgh, PA)
Jones (Smithton, PA)
Latrobe Brewing (Latrobe, PA)
Genesee (Rochester, NY)
Anheuser-Busch (Baldwinsville, NY)
West End (Utica, NY)

Anheuser-Busch (Merrimack, NH)
Boston Beer Co (Boston, MA)

Cold Spring Brewing (Cold Spring, MN)
Stroh (St Paul, MN)
Heileman (St Paul, MN)
Hibernia (Eau Clare, WI)
Heileman (La Crosse, WI)
Huber (Monroe, WI)

Miller (Milwaukee)
Pabst (Milwaukee)

Anheuser-Busch (Newark, NJ)
Lion (Wilkes-Barre, PA)
Schaefer (Stroh) (Allentown, PA)
Yuengling (Pottsville, PA)
Eastern Brewing (Hammonton, NJ)
Heileman (Baltimore, MD)

Falstaff (Fort Wayne, IN)

Anheuser-Busch (Columbus, OH)

Hudepohl-Schoennling (Cincinnati, OH)

Anheuser-Busch (Williamsburg, VA)

Heileman (Evansville, IN)

Heileman (Belleville, IL)
Anheuser-Busch (St Louis, MO)

Miller (Eden, NC)
Stroh (Winston-Salem, NC)

Stroh (Memphis, TN)

Heileman (Perry, GA)

Miller (Fort Worth, TX)

Miller (Albany, GA)

Stroh (Longview, TX)

Anheuser-Busch (Jacksonville, FL)

Pearl (San Antonio, TX)
Lone Star (Heileman) (San Antonio, TX)

Dixie (New Orleans, LA)

Anheuser-Busch (Tampa, FL)

Anheuser-Busch (Houston, TX)

Note: Breweries with an annual production under 100,000 barrels are indicated
but not named.

include Pabst Light, Buckhorn, Hamm's, Jacob Best Premium Light and MAXX Special Lager. The Pabst-owned Olympia Brewery at Tumwater brews Olympia (aka 'Oly'), Olympia Light and Gold Light. Pabst was itself taken over in February 1985 by the late California millionaire Paul Kalmanovitz, who already owned the Falstaff, General and Pearl breweries.

Falstaff Brewing of Fort Wayne, Indiana, traces its roots to the Forest Park Brewing Company of St Louis, Missouri, that was established in 1910 and taken over by 'Papa Joe' Griesdieck in 1917. Renamed Falstaff (after the Shakespeare character) during Prohibition, the company expanded to

become one of the Midwest's strongest multisite regional brewers. After World War II, Falstaff became a leading national brewer. After the 1960s, however, Falstaff's market position gave way to other brands such as Miller and Coors, and many of the company's breweries were sold or closed.

The number of brewing companies declined rapidly during the 1950s and 1960s, and remained relatively constant in the 1970s. However, since the beginning of the 1980s, the brewing industry in the United States has been enjoying a renaissance. After four decades of decline in the number of brewers, well over one hundred microbreweries and brewpubs have opened their doors.

Inspired by Fritz Maytag's extraordinary success with San Francisco's Anchor Brewing, the microbrewery revolution began in California but soon spread across the nation. Anchor Brewing Company was originally established in San Francisco in 1896. Appliance heir Fritz Maytag bought the company in 1965 when it was on the verge of collapse and turned it into the very model of an efficient, smaller regional brewery. During his first two decades, Maytag increased the brewery's output 75-fold! The company's flagship product is Anchor Steam Beer, one of America's most prized premium beers, which was developed by master brewer Maytag himself, and is loosely based on what is

SOUTHERN REGIONALS

Abita Brewing was founded in the town of Abita Springs, Louisiana, in 1986.

Dixie Brewing of New Orleans was established in 1907 and was, until recently, the only remaining brewery in the Louisiana city that once was the brewing capital of the entire South.

Spoetzl Brewery of Shiner, Texas, evolved from the Shiner Brewing Association started in 1909, and was taken over by the Petzold and Spoetzl partnership in 1915. In 1989, the company was purchased by Gambrinus Imports, the San Antonio-based importer of Modelo's Corona brand.

ABOVE: Jim Koch, the founder of the Boston Beer Co, and creator of Samuel Adams ales and lagers.

known of the legendary 'steam' beers produced in gold rush days. Other Anchor products include Anchor Porter, Anchor Liberty Ale, Old Foghorn Barley Wine-style Ale, which was first produced in 1975. Anchor is renowned locally for its annual Christmas beer, which has been specially brewed since 1975, with a different recipe each year.

Among the important early microbrewery pioneers were Sierra Nevada Brewing in California (1980), Boulder Brewing in Colorado (1980), Mendocino Brewing in California (1982), Yakima Brewing in Washington (1982), Buffalo Bill's in California (1983) and Widmer Brewing in Oregon (1984). Mike McMenamin of Portland, Oregon, opened his first brewpub in 1985 and now owns a chain of over a dozen.

Meanwhile, on the East Coast in 1985, Jim Koch had his recipe for Samuel Adams lager produced under contract, and an extensive market for his beer was well established by the time that he actually began brewing in Boston in 1987. Initially, Koch's flagship brand, Samuel Adams Boston Lager, was available only in Boston, Massachusetts, and Munich, Germany, but is now in nationwide distribution in the United States. After having had his beer contract brewed by Pittsburgh Brewing for two years, Koch moved production to a renovated 40,000-barrel

(48,000-hectoliter) brewery in Boston in 1987. The brewery's other brands include Samuel Adams Double Bock and Boston Lightship.

By definition, a *microbrewery* was originally a brewery with a capacity of less than 3000 barrels (2500 hectoliters), but by the end of the 1980s this threshold was increased to 15,000 barrels (12,500 hectoliters) as the demand for microbrewed beer doubled and then tripled. A *brewpub* is, by definition, a pub or tavern that brews its own beer on the premises. Until the 1980s, as a holdover from Prohibition laws, it was illegal in most states and Canadian provinces to both brew beer and sell it directly to the public on the same site. Subsequent changes in local laws have rescinded these outdated restrictions and have made it possible for brewpubs to flourish. Ironically, brewpubs were once very much a part of American history. During the seventeenth century many of the original establishments in places such as New Amsterdam were, in fact, brewpubs.

A brewpub differs from a microbrewery in that its primary market is under its own roof. Some brewpubs bottle their beers for sale to patrons and for wholesale to retailers, while some microbreweries also operate

Some Regional Brewers In The Mountain West

Albuquerque Brewing & Bottling is a brewpub in Albuquerque, New Mexico.

Aspen Beer Company was founded in 1988 in Aspen, Colorado. Its Aspen Silver City Ale is brewed under contract at Boulder Brewing.

Bayern Brewing operates the Northern Pacific Brewpub, an establishment with a predictably Bavarian theme, opened in August 1987 in the former Northern Pacific Railway station in Missoula, Montana.

Boulder Brewing Company of Boulder, Colorado, which began operations in 1980, is the second largest Colorado-based brewer after Coors.

Carver's is a brewpub that opened in 1988 in Durango, Colorado, offering ales as well as a stout and Wheat & Honey beer.

Coeur d'Alene Brewing operates 'TW Fishers, A Brewpub,' which opened in Coeur d'Alene, Idaho, in July 1987, three weeks after brewpubs officially became legal in Idaho.

Montana Beverages of Helena, Montana, was established in 1982 by Dick Burke and Bruce DeRosier to brew beer under the Kessler brand name. It was first produced in 1984 and is a reference to the original Kessler brewery, which was started in 1865 by Luxembourg native Nick Kessler and later grew into one of Montana's most important breweries. Today the brewery produces the Kessler brand beers, as well as brewing under contract for companies in Eugene, Oregon, Santa Barbara, California, and Jackson Hole, Wyoming.

New Belgium is a Ft Collins, Colorado, microbrewery specializing in beers based on traditional Belgian styles including cherry beer, and ales in the style of the Trappist abbeys.

Odell Brewing is a microbrewery in Ft Collins, Colorado, which brews a variety of ales including Easy Street Wheat, a wheat ale that won a gold medal at the 1993 Great American Beer Festival.

Schirf Brewing, located in Park City, Utah, is the only brewery to operate in Utah since 1967. Founded as a microbrewery in October 1986, Schirf expanded into its Wasatch brewpub in July 1989.

Sun Valley Brewing is a microbrewery located in the town of Wood River, Idaho, near the Sun Valley ski resort. The brewery has been in operation since November 1986, and the principal brands brewed here are Our Holiday Ale, Sawtooth Gold Lager, White Cloud Ale and Yule Ale.

Table Rock is a brewpub that opened in Boise, Idaho, in 1991.

The Walnut Brewery is a brewpub which opened in Boulder, Colorado, in 1990 and produces a variety of ales as well as Devil's Thumb Stout.

SOME CALIFORNIA BREWERS

Alpine Village Hofbräu, a brewpub which opened during 1988 in the city of Torrance, is partly owned by the Hofbräuhaus Traunstein in Bavaria.

Over three decades Anchor Brewing of San Francisco has evolved as one of America's premier mid-size brewers, and a model for the microbrewery movement.

Anderson Valley Brewing of Booneville operates a brewpub called The Buckhorn Saloon, a successor to the original Buckhorn Saloon that was established in 1873.

Belmont Brewing opened in Long Beach, in 1990.

Buffalo Bill's of Hayward became one of the first three brewpubs to open in the United States since Prohibition when brewmaster Bill Owens opened for business in September 1983. In 1988, Owens opened a second brewpub, Bison Brewing Company, in nearby Berkeley, which has since been sold.

Crown City Brewery is a microbrewery that opened in Pasadena in July 1988.

Golden Pacific Brewing is a microbrewery begun in 1985 in Emeryville. In 1989, Golden Pacific signed an agreement with Thousand Oaks Brewing to begin producing their products in Emeryville.

Humboldt Brewery is a brewpub located in the town of Arcata.

Mad River Brewing Company of Blue Lake was founded by veteran brewmaster Bob Smith in 1989. Mad River is noted for its flagship brand, Steelhead Extra Pale Ale.

Opened in 1993, Manhattan Beach Brewing also brews pale ale, a wheat ale, a raspberry ale and stout.

Marin Brewing Company of Larkspur (Marin County), was founded in April 1989 by brewmaster Brendan Moylan.

Mendocino Brewing in Hopland was founded by Michael Laybourn, Norman Franks and John Scahill in 1982. It was California's first brewpub since Prohibition and produces about 8000 barrels (9500 hectoliters) a year. Its brands are typically named for birds of the region and include Black Hawk Stout, Blue Heron Pale Ale, Eye of the Hawk, Peregrine Pale Ale and Red Tail Ale.

Napa Valley Brewing of Calistoga also operates the historic 1882 Calistoga Inn, a brewpub, restaurant and hotel. A brewery located in the heart of North America's premier wine-producing region may seem to be out of place, but

FAR RIGHT: The Golden Bear lagers of Golden Pacific.

RIGHT: The bar at North Coast Brewing in Fort Bragg.

Napa Valley Brewing's beers are just as world class as the wines being produced from the adjacent fields.

Nevada City Brewing, a tiny sister brewery to Truckee Brewing, is located in Nevada City.

North Coast Brewing was founded in Fort Bragg on California's Mendocino County coast in 1988, and produces Red Seal Ale, Scrimshaw Pilsner Style Beer and Old No 45 Stout, as well as seasonal brews.

Oakland's Pacific Coast Brewing has been producing ales and stouts since 1988.

Rubicon Brewing is a microbrewery located in the city of Sacramento, with brewing under the direction of master brewer Phil Moeller.

San Andreas Brewing operates the Earthquake Country brewpub that opened in Hollister in September 1988. Named for California's San Andreas fault, which is not actually near Hollister, the brewery's principal draft brands were named with an 'earthquake' theme. They include Earthquake Pale, Earthquake Porter, Kit Fox Amber and Seismic Ale.

San Francisco Brewing Company is located on the site of the historic Albatross Saloon on Columbus Avenue in San Francisco. America's fourth brewpub, brewing began here in November 1986 under the direction of owner and master brewer Allen Paul.

Santa Cruz Brewing brews and bottles beer for the local, northern California market and operates the Front Street Pub in Santa Cruz. The principal brands brewed here are Lighthouse Amber, Lighthouse Lager and Pacific Porter.

Since 1990, Shields Brewing, a brewpub in Ventura, has been producing Channel Islands ales and stouts.

Sierra Nevada Brewing of Chico was founded in 1980 by Paul Camus and Ken Grossman as one of the nation's first microbreweries. As of 1989, Sierra Nevada's brewing capacity was 50,000 barrels (59,000 hectoliters), up from 10,000 barrels (11,900 hectoliters) in 1987, making it one of the largest microbreweries in the United States.

Stanislaus Brewing of Modesto was established by Garith Helm, who began commercial production in 1984. The 'patron saint' of Stanislaus Brewing is 'St Stan,' a public relations man who assumes the character of a brewer named Brother Stanislaus, who is said to have brewed a beer inspired by divine intervention for Frederick the Great. Stanislaus Brewing produces only altbier, a German-style, top-fermented brew similar to ale.

SOME NORTHWESTERN REGIONAL BREWERS

Alaskan Brewing & Bottling (formerly Chinook Alaskan) is located in the town of Douglas, near Juneau, Alaska. Established in 1986, it is the first brewery to be built in Alaska since Prinzbräu folded in 1979.

BridgePort Brewing is a brewpub located in the city of Portland, Oregon.

The Deschutes Brewery is a brewpub opened in Bend, Oregon, in 1989 and noted for a variety of ales as well as porter and stout.

Originally founded in Ft Spokane, Washington, by the Bockemuehl brothers in 1889, the Ft Spokane Brewery was reopened in 1989, specializing in German-style alt biers.

Hales Ales, Ltd is a microbrewery located in Colville, Washington, north of Spokane, that was established in 1984.

Hart Brewing Company of Kalama, Washington, north of Vancouver, is one of the many microbreweries that sprang up in the Pacific Northwest during 1984 and 1985.

Hood River Brewing and its adjacent White Cap Pub opened in 1987 in the town of Hood River, Oregon. Full Sail Ale won a gold medal at the 1989 Great American Beer Festival.

Kemper Brewing on Bainbridge Island in Washington's Puget Sound is another of the microbreweries founded in the Pacific Northwest in 1984.

Mike McMenamin of Portland, Oregon, and his brother Brian operate more than a dozen restaurants and pubs in Oregon, including six brewpubs, making the McMenamin group the largest *chain* brewpubs in the United States.

Pike Place Brewery is a microbrewery which opened in the historic Pike Place Market in Seattle, Washington, in October 1989. It is owned jointly by internationally known beer importer Charles Finkel and brewmaster John Farias, who oversees the brewing of Pike Place Pale Ale and other specialty beers.

Redhook Ale Brewery of Seattle, Washington, was established by Paul Shipman in 1982 in the city's Ballard district. Brands include Redhook Ale, Blackhook Porter, Ballard Bitter and Winterhook Christmas Ale.

Roslyn Brewing of Roslyn, Washington, was originally founded in 1889 (some sources say 1891) by William Dewitt and Frank Groger. Closed in 1915 prior to Prohibition, Roslyn Brewing was re-established in its centennial year by Roger Beardsley and Dino Enrico.

Widmer Brewing of Portland, Oregon, was established by Kurt Widmer in 1984. It was the second microbrewery to be established in Portland and is the largest microbrewery in Oregon, a state noted for its vast proliferation of small breweries. In addition to Widmer Altbier, the brewery also produces Widmer Weizen, Hefeweizen and seasonal brews such as Bock, Oktoberfest, Festbier and Märzen.

Yakima Brewing & Malting is a microbrewery established in 1982 in Yakima, Washington, in the heart of North America's greatest hop-growing region. Under the direction of founder Herbert Grant, the brewery produces beer for both the retail market and for Grant's own brewpub.

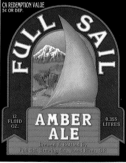

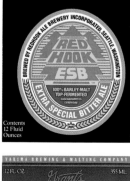

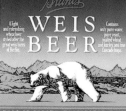

brewpubs, so the distinction between the two is somewhat blurred. Both, however, share a commitment to their own unique beers, and most brewpublicans entered their trade out of a love for brewing and an interest in distinctive beer styles.

Inspired by Fritz Maytag's Anchor Brewing, the microbrewery revolution started with the now extinct New Albion Brewing of Sonoma, California, which was founded by Jack McAuliffe in 1976. At the same time that McAuliffe was starting New Albion, there was a growing public awareness of beer styles, such as ales, wheat beers and stouts, that were rare or even unknown in the United States, and imports were becoming increasingly popular, particularly in major cities such as Seattle, Portland, San Francisco and New York. Indeed, it was this interest in European beer styles, nurtured in the 1970s, that was a catalyst for the microbreweries of the 1980s. It also became common to see as many as one dozen draft handles in a tavern.

Although today the area stretching south from western Oregon and Washington to the San Francisco Bay Area contains the largest concentration of brewpubs and microbreweries in North America, the revolution has spread to every corner of the continent—from Florida Brewing in Miami, to the Granite Brewery in Halifax, Nova Scotia; to Schirf Brewing in Park City, Utah, to Alaskan Brewing (formerly Chinook) in Douglas, Alaska. Milwaukee, once the proud capital of American brewing, experienced the demise of both Schlitz and Blatz, but now has the Lakefront and Sprecher microbreweries.

The major national brands in the United States, Canada and Mexico all produce more beer in a week than microbreweries do in a year, but the microbreweries have had the effect of enriching the overall brewing scene and have prompted the majors to rethink their notions about super premium beers. Certainly this will be part of the legacy of the microbrewery revolution that will be carried forward into the final years of the century.

The spectrum of beer styles being brewed today is nothing short of incredible, compared to what was available even as recently as 1980. Not only is there the best selection of lagers in over half a century, but Americans are able to choose from ales and wheat beers, and brewers are producing distinctive stouts and have even helped to revive the art of porter brewing, which had all but died out even in England. American brewers are also developing more esoteric beer styles. Best of all, the United States now has fresh local beers of every style for those who desire a more flavorful alternative to mass market lagers.

ABOVE: Hops! is a chain of three brewpubs in Scottsdale, Arizona (opened in 1990); La Jolla, California (1992); and Phoenix, Arizona (1994).

BELOW: Opened in 1993, San Diego Brewing is a microbrewery based on the tradition of the brewery of the same name that existed here from 1896 to 1942.

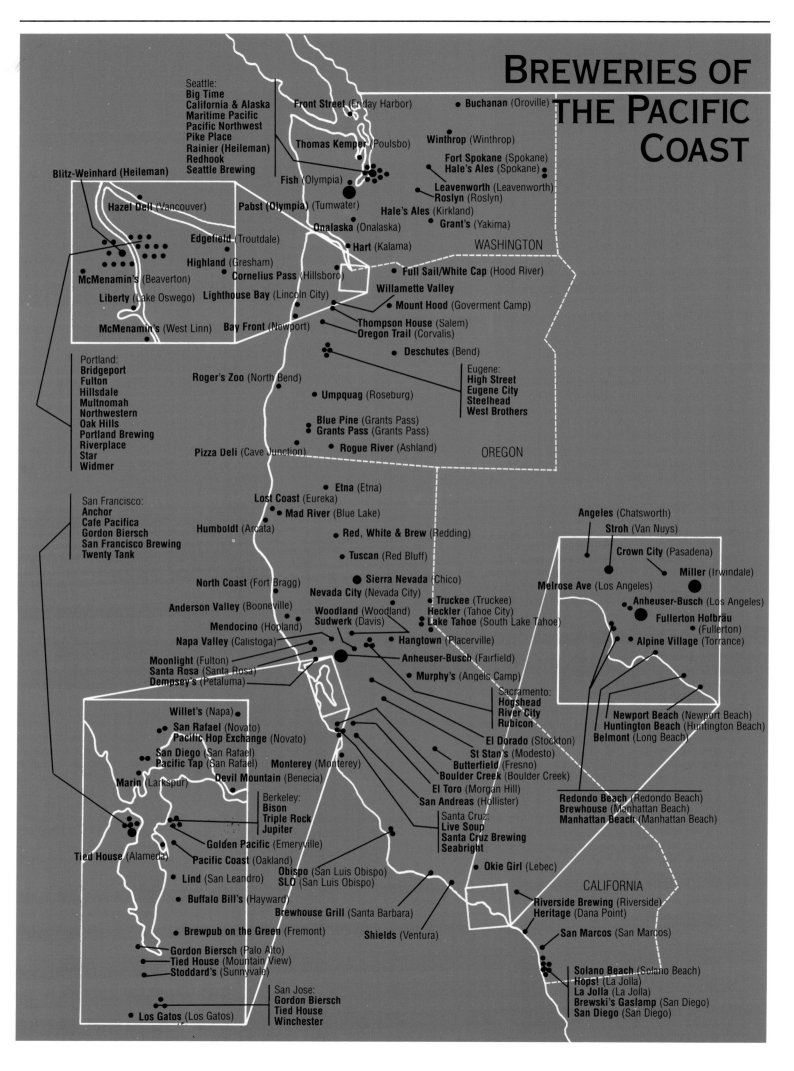

BREWERIES OF THE PACIFIC COAST

Seattle:
Big Time
California & Alaska
Maritime Pacific
Pacific Northwest
Pike Place
Rainier (Heileman)
Redhook
Seattle Brewing

Front Street (Friday Harbor)

Buchanan (Oroville)

Winthrop (Winthrop)

Thomas Kemper (Poulsbo)

Fort Spokane (Spokane)
Hale's Ales (Spokane)

Blitz-Weinhard (Heileman)

Leavenworth (Leavenworth)
Roslyn (Roslyn)

Fish (Olympia)

Hazel Dell (Vancouver)

Pabst (Olympia) (Tumwater)

Hale's Ales (Kirkland)

Grant's (Yakima)

Edgefield (Troutdale)

Onalaska (Onalaska)

WASHINGTON

Highland (Gresham)

Hart (Kalama)

Cornelius Pass (Hillsboro)

Full Sail/White Cap (Hood River)

McMenamin's (Beaverton)

Willamette Valley

Liberty (Lake Oswego)

Lighthouse Bay (Lincoln City)

Mount Hood (Goverment Camp)

McMenamin's (West Linn)

Bay Front (Newport)

Thompson House (Salem)
Oregon Trail (Corvalis)

Portland:
Bridgeport
Fulton
Hillsdale
Multnomah
Northwestern
Oak Hills
Portland Brewing
Riverplace
Star
Widmer

Deschutes (Bend)

Eugene:
High Street
Eugene City
Steelhead
West Brothers

Roger's Zoo (North Bend)

Umpquag (Roseburg)

Blue Pine (Grants Pass)
Grants Pass (Grants Pass)

Pizza Deli (Cave Junction)

Rogue River (Ashland)

OREGON

Etna (Etna)

San Francisco:
Anchor
Cafe Pacifica
Gordon Biersch
San Francisco Brewing
Twenty Tank

Lost Coast (Eureka)

Mad River (Blue Lake)

Humboldt (Arcata)

Red, White & Brew (Redding)

Tuscan (Red Bluff)

Angeles (Chatsworth)

Stroh (Van Nuys)

Crown City (Pasadena)

Miller (Irwindale)

North Coast (Fort Bragg)

Sierra Nevada (Chico)

Melrose Ave (Los Angeles)

Nevada City (Nevada City)

Anheuser-Busch (Los Angeles)

Anderson Valley (Booneville)

Truckee (Truckee)
Heckler (Tahoe City)

Fullerton Hofbräu (Fullerton)

Woodland (Woodland)
Sudwerk (Davis)

Lake Tahoe (South Lake Tahoe)

Mendocino (Hopland)

Hangtown (Placerville)

Alpine Village (Torrance)

Napa Valley (Calistoga)

Moonlight (Fulton)
Santa Rosa (Santa Rosa)
Dempsey's (Petaluma)

Anheuser-Busch (Fairfield)

Murphy's (Angels Camp)

Sacramento:
Hogshead
River City
Rubicon

Newport Beach (Newport Beach)
Huntington Beach (Huntington Beach)
Belmont (Long Beach)

Willet's (Napa)

San Rafael (Novato)
Pacific Hop Exchange (Novato)

El Dorado (Stockton)
St Stan's (Modesto)
Butterfield (Fresno)

San Diego (San Rafael)
Pacific Tap (San Rafael)

Monterey (Monterey)

Boulder Creek (Boulder Creek)
El Toro (Morgan Hill)
San Andreas (Hollister)

Marin (Larkspur)

Devil Mountain (Benecia)

Berkeley:
Bison
Triple Rock
Jupiter

Santa Cruz:
Live Soup
Santa Cruz Brewing
Seabright

Redondo Beach (Redondo Beach)
Brewhouse (Manhattan Beach)
Manhattan Beach (Manhattan Beach)

Golden Pacific (Emeryville)

Tied House (Alameda)

Pacific Coast (Oakland)

Obispo (San Luis Obispo)
SLO (San Luis Obispo)

Okie Girl (Lebec)

Lind (San Leandro)

Buffalo Bill's (Hayward)

Brewhouse Grill (Santa Barbara)

CALIFORNIA

Brewpub on the Green (Fremont)

Shields (Ventura)

Riverside Brewing (Riverside)
Heritage (Dana Point)

Gordon Biersch (Palo Alto)
Tied House (Mountain View)
Stoddard's (Sunnyvale)

San Marcos (San Marcos)

San Jose:
Gordon Biersch
Tied House
Winchester

Solano Beach (Solano Beach)
Hops! (La Jolla)
La Jolla (La Jolla)
Brewski's Gaslamp (San Diego)
San Diego (San Diego)

Los Gatos (Los Gatos)

GLOSSARY

Ale: A top-fermented beer that originated in England as early as the seventh century and made with hops after the sixteenth century. It is fermented at temperatures ranging between 55 degrees F and 70 degrees F (13 degrees C and 21 degrees C), somewhat warmer than those used to ferment lager. It is the primary beer type in England and among North American microbreweries, but extremely rare elsewhere. It is, however, a close cousin to the German **altbier.** Subtypes include pale ale (which is actually much more amber than pale lagers), brown ale and India pale ale, a beer developed in the nineteenth century by English brewers for export to the Empire.

Altbier: The German equivalent of English or American 'ale,' literally a beer made in the 'old' way (pre-nineteenth century) with top-fermenting yeast. It is indigenous to Dusseldorf, Germany, and environs. Virtually unknown in the United States after Prohibition, it was reintroduced by several microbreweries in Oregon and California during the 1980s.

Alus: The Latvian word for beer.

Barley Wine: In Britain, ales with alcohol contents approaching that of wine (up to and surpassing 10 percent by volume) are called barley wines.

Barrel: A container for beer, at one time made of reinforced oak, now made solely of stainless steel. Also a unit of measuring beer which equals 31 gallons, or 1.2 hectoliters.

Beer: A general term for *all* fermented malt beverages flavored with hops. The term embraces ale, lager, porter, stout and all other types discussed herein. Ingredients include malted cereal grains (especially, but not limited to, barley), hops, yeast and water, although early English beers were unhopped. Subtypes are classified by whether they are made with top-fermenting yeast (ale, porter, stout, wheat beer) or bottom-fermenting yeast (lager, bock beer, malt liquor). Generally, top-fermented beers are darker, ranging from a translucent copper to opaque brown, while bottom-fermented beers range from amber to pale yellow. Because of their English heritage, top-fermented beers are usually drunk at room temperature, while bottom-fermented beers are served cold.

Bier: The German, Dutch and Flemish word for beer.

Bière: The French word for beer.

Birra: The Italian word for beer.

Bitter: A full-bodied, highly hopped ale (hence the name) that is extremely popular in England but much less so elsewhere. Bitter (or bitter ale) is similar in color to other ales, but it lacks carbonation and has a slightly higher alcohol content.

A noun used in England to identify highly-hopped ale. Originally it was probably short for bitter ale. The less-used antonym is 'mild,' also a noun, which implies a lightly hopped English ale.

Bock Beer: A bottom-fermented beer that is darker than lager and which has a relatively higher alcohol content, usually in the six percent range. Bock originated in Germany and most German brewers still brew it as a special supplement to their principal product line. An especially strong, dark lager occasionally, but not necessarily, produced in concordance with spring festivals. A seasonal beer, it is traditionally associated with spring festivals. Prior to World War II, many American brewers produced a bock beer each spring, but the advent of national marketing after the war largely eliminated the practice of brewing seasonal beers. In the 1980s, several breweries reintroduced bock beer. The male goat (*bock* in German) is the traditional symbol of bock beer. Subtypes include **doppelbock,** a bock especially high in alcohol, and **maibock,** a bock marketed in conjunction with May festivals.

Brasserie: The French word for brewery, also for a small café.

Bräuerei: The German word for brewery.

Brewing: Generically, the entire beer-making process, but technically only that part of the process during which the beer wort is cooked in a brew kettle and during which time the hops are added. After brewing, the beer is fermented. (See **Fermentation.**)

Brewpub: A brewpub is, by definition, a pub or tavern that brews its own beer on the premises. Until the 1980s, as a holdover from Prohibition laws, it was illegal in most states and Canadian provinces to both brew beer and sell it directly to the public on the same site. Subsequent changes in local laws have rescinded these outdated restrictions and have made it possible for brewpubs to become more widespread. A brewpub differs from a **microbrewery** in that its primary market is under its own roof. Some brewpubs bottle their beers for sale to patrons and for wholesale to retailers, while some microbreweries also operate brewpubs, so the distinction between the two is somewhat blurred. Both, however,

THE INNER WORKINGS OF A MODERN BREWHOUSE

In this illustration, courtesy of Luxembourg's Brasserie Nationale, we see the specific steps of the brewing process. The technical terminology is explained in greater detail in the adjacent pages of the Glossary.

(1) Barley or other grain, which has been malted, is usually stored in the highest portion of the brewhouse, so that it can feed by gravity into the brewing process. Before brewing it is ground into finer particles known as grist.

(2) The exact mineral content of the water used in brewing is carefully considered.

(3) Malted grist is mixed with hot water in the mash tun where it is processed by mixing rakes. It is here that starches become fermentable sugars. (3a) Some brewers use a two-step mashing process.

(4) The mixture or mash passes to the lauter tun where it is clarified and spent grain is extracted for use as livestock feed.

(5) The liquid from the lauter tun, known as wort, passes to the brew kettle where it is boiled and flavored with hops. Technically, this is the step known as 'brewing.'

NOTE: The brewing vessels such as the mash tun (3), lauter tun (4) and brew kettle (5) are traditionally made of copper, but many modern brewhouses use stainless steel vessels.

(6) The hopped wort passes through a heat exchanger, or plate cooler, where it is cooled.

(7) (8) The cooled wort is aerated and yeast is added to begin fermentation.

(9) Primary fermentation may take place in tall stainless steel tanks (seen here) or in large open trays.

(10) After primary fermentation, the beer goes into closed tanks for secondary fermentation. For ales using top-fermenting yeast, this step is a matter of days. For lagers using bottom-fermenting yeast, the beer is stored (in German 'lagered') for about a month or so.

(11) (12) At this point the fermented beer may or may not be filtered and/or pasteurized (hefewiess and some ales are specifically not filtered); and (13) pressurized. The beer is now ready for packaging in bottles, cans or kegs.

(14) Bottles are cleaned, (15) filled, (16) capped and (17) labeled.

(18) Kegs are cleaned, (19) filled and (20) prepared for delivery to the consumer.

share a commitment to their own unique beers, and most brewpublicans entered their trade out of a love for brewing and an interest in distinctive beer styles.

Brouwerij: The Dutch and Flemish word for brewery.

Cervecería: The Spanish word for brewery.

Cerveja: The Portuguese word for beer.

Cervejaria: The Portuguese word for brewery.

Cerveza: The Spanish word for beer.

Cream Ale: A blend of ale and lager invented in the early twentieth century by American brewers.

Diat: A German word for lager low in carbohydrates originally developed for diabetics. It is *not* a 'diet' or low-calorie beer.

Doppelbock: A German word literally meaning 'double bock.' Although it is not nearly twice as strong as **bock**, it is typically the highest alcohol (over seven percent by volume) beer style brewed in Germany but lower in alcohol than English **barley wine**. In naming practice, doppelbocks are given names ending in 'ator,' such as Celebrator, Salvator or Optimator.

Draft (Draught) Beer: A term which literally means beer that is drawn from a keg rather than packaged in bottles or cans. Designed for immediate use, draft beer is not pasteurized and hence must be kept cold to prevent the loss of its fresh taste. Draft beer is generally better than packaged beer when fresh but not so as it ages. Some brewers sell unpasteurized draft-style beer in cans and bottles, which must be shipped in refrigerated containers.

Dry Beer: A pale lager in which all the fermentable sugars from the original malt have been converted to alcohol. In order to conclude the process with a beer of acceptable alcohol content (roughly 3.2 percent by weight), a brewer must start with less malt. Hence, dry beer has a low original gravity and will have very little flavor unless it is more heavily hopped than typical beers. The process is similar to that used by brewers to produce light beer, and the results are very similar. In fact, most American mass market lagers, including light and dry beers, are very similar in taste. Beer in which all fermentable sugars are fermented was developed in Germany and Switzerland in the 1970s as **diat** beer, a beer designed for diabetics.

ABOVE: Filtration tanks at Steiererbräu in Austria.

Dunkel (Dunkles): A German adjective used to describe a dark lager, usually in the sweeter Munich style.

Eisbock: A German term that originated in Dortmund and applied to especially flavorful and powerful light-colored lagers.

Export: This style evolved when the brewers in Dortmund, Germany, began transporting beer to other markets across the continent. In order to withstand the rigors of travel, they produced a beer that was well hopped and slightly higher in alcohol. As such, the Dortmund lager as a style is known as 'export.' Dortmunder lagers are traditionally full-bodied but not quite as sweet as the beers of Munich, though not as dry as a true Pilsner. Beers identified as such are not necessarily brewed specifically to be exported, although they often are.

Faro: A light, sweet Belgian lambic favored in Brussels.

Fermentation: The process by which yeast turns the sugars present in malted grains into alcohol and carbon dioxide. Chem-ically, the process is written as:

$$C_6 H_{12} O_6 \rightarrow 2\ C_2 H_5 OH + 2\ CO_2$$
(glucose)   (alcohol)   (carbon
                                              dioxide)

Framboise/Frambozen: A Belgian lambic flavored with raspberries.

Gueuze: Blended Belgian lambic beers not containing fruits.

Hell (Helles): An adjective used to describe lager that is pale in color.

Hops: The dried blossom of the female hop plant which is a climbing herb (*Humulus lupulus*) native to temperate regions of the Northern Hemisphere and cultivated in Europe, the United Kingdom and the United States. Belonging to the mulberry family, the hop's leaves and flowers are characterized by a bitter taste and aroma. It has been used since the ninth century as the principal flavoring and seasoning agent in brewing, although it had been prized before that for its medicinal properties. In addition to its aromatic resins, the hop also contains tannin which helps to clarify beer.

Different strains of hops have different properties and much of the brewmaster's art is in knowing how to use these properties. For example, one strain may be particularly bitter to the taste without being very aromatic, while another strain might be just the opposite. The brewmaster will blend the two in various combinations just as a chef will experiment with various seasonings before settling on just the right combination for a particular recipe. Hops also serve as a natural preservative.

Ice Beer: Developed and patented by Labatt in Canada, ice beer is a pale lager which is quickly chilled to sub-freezing temperatures after brewing but before final fermentation. The result is the formation of ice crystals in the beer, which are removed to produce a beer with roughly *twice* the alcohol content of typical mass market lagers.

Keller: A German-style of packaged, unfiltered lager that emulates *vom fass* (on draft) beer.

Krausening (Kraeusening): The process of instigating a secondary fermentation to produce additional carbon dioxide in a beer. Some brewers will first ferment their beer in open containers where alcohol is produced and retained, but the carbon dioxide escapes. The second fermentation, or krausening, then takes place in closed containers after a first fermentation (whether that first fermentation took place in open or closed containers) and is used to produce natural carbonation or sparkle in the beer.

Kriek: A Belgian lambic flavored with cherries. Probably the most popular of the fruit lambics.

Lager: This beer style accounts for well over 90 percent of the beer brewed and marketed in the world (outside England). Specifically, it is a clear, pale beer fermented with bottom-fermenting yeast at nearly freezing temperatures. The fermentation period is also longer than that for ale and hence the name, which is German meaning 'to store.' Lager had its origins in the heart of central Europe in an area that the author likes to call the Golden Triangle. This triangle is so named because of the golden color of lager itself and because of the success that brewers had with this product when it was first developed for widespread commercial sale in the early to middle nineteenth century. The corners of the Triangle lie in Munich, Prague and Vienna, the capitals, respectively, of Bavaria (a state of the German Federal Republic), Bohemia (Czech Republic) and Austria.

Lambic: A style of beer fermented with special strains of wild yeast indigenous only to Belgium's Senne Valley. One of the world's most unique native beer styles.

Lautering: The process of straining wort in a lauter tun before it is cooked in the brew kettle.

Lauter Tun: The vessel used in brewing between the mash tun and the brew kettle. It separates the barley husks from the clear liquid wort. The barley husks themselves help provide a natural filter bed through which the wort is strained.

Leicht: The German word for 'light,' or low-calorie beer.

Light Beer: Introduced in the mid-1970s by nearly every major brewer in the United States and Canada, light beers are by definition reduced-calorie lagers or ales. They also have a slightly lower alcohol content than comparable lagers or ales.

Maibock: A bock beer brewed for release in May.

Malt Liquor: A bottom-fermented beer, it has a malty taste more closely related to top-fermented ale than to lager which is bottom-fermented. Malt liquor has a much higher alcohol content (5.6 to 6.5 percent) than lager.

A term imposed by the American government to identify beer with an alcohol content above five percent. It is not actually a true beer type as the term may be imposed on ales or lagers. Some larger American brewers produce very pale high-alcohol lagers and call them malt liquors.

Malting: The process by which barley kernels are moistened and germinated, producing a 'green malt' which is then dried. This renders the starches present in the kernel soluble. If pale beers are to be produced, the malt is simply dried. If dark beers are to be produced, the malt is roasted until it is dark brown. The malt is then subjected to mashing.

Mash: The substance that is produced by mashing.

Mashing: The process by which barley malt is mixed with water and cooked to turn soluble starch into fermentable sugar. Other cereal grains, such as corn and rice, many also be added (rice contributes to a paler end product beer). After mashing in a mash tun, the mash is filtered through a lauter tun, whereupon it becomes known as wort.

Microbrewery: By definition, a microbrewery was originally considered to be a brewery with a capacity of less than 3000 barrels (2500 hectoliters), but by the end of the 1980s this threshold increased to 15,000 barrels (12,500 hectoliters) as the demand for microbrewed beer doubled and then *tripled.* A **brewpub** is, by definition, a pub or tavern that brews its own beer on the premises.

Märzen: Originally this German term was used to describe a reddish lager brewed in March and set aside for summer. The style is now brewed for autumn consumption, particularly in connection with Oktoberfest.

Near Beer: Non-alcoholic beer which originated during the Prohibition era in the United States and which is still in production.

Ol: The Danish, Norwegian and Swedish word for beer.

Olut: The Finnish word for beer.

Pasteurization: Though this term has come to mean the heating of a substance to kill harmful bacteria, the process was originally proposed by Louis Pasteur as a means of killing yeast to end fermentation and hence end the creation of alcohol and carbon dioxide (carbonation). Nonpasteurized beers are no less sanitary than pasteurized beers.

Pêche: A Belgian lambic flavored with peaches that has become increasingly popular in recent years.

Pils: A German term for pale, Pilsen-style lagers.

Pilsener or Pilsner: A pale, bottom-fermented lager beer originally associated with the city of Pilsen, Bohemia (Czech Republic), where it was first brewed in the early nineteenth century. The term is often used interchangeably with the term lager, although pilsners are technically the palest of lagers. Pilsners are the most widely known and widely imitated lager type. The Plzensky Prazdroj brewery in Pilsen brews Pilsner Urquell ('Pilsner from the original source'), which is considered the definitive pilsner, although the term has become generic.

Pivo: The Czech word for beer.

Piwo: The Polish word for beer.

Porter: A dark, sweet beer brewed with top-fermenting (ale type) yeast that was developed in London in the late eighteenth century and revived by American microbrewers in the late twentieth century. It took its name from the city's porters who had taken an immediate fancy to it. Similar to but sweeter than stout, it is a dark beer of moderate strength (five to seven percent alcohol by volume), made with roasted unmalted barley.

Prohibition: The process by which a government prohibits its citizens from buying or possessing alcoholic beverages. Specifically, *the* Prohibition refers to the period between the effective date of the 18th Amendment to the US Constitution (16 January 1920) and its repeal by the 21st Amendment. Repeal took effect on 5 December 1933, although it passed Congress in February and the sale of beer was permitted after 7 April 1933.

Rauchbier: A lager with a wonderfully smoky flavor which uses malted grain that has been roasted over a very smoky beechwood fire. Indigenous to the Bamberg area in southern Germany, rauchbier means literally 'smoked beer.' As such, the grain is not only roasted to a dark color, but it takes on a distinctive smoky flavor as well. Smoked beer, which is rare outside of Germany, is generally served with meals including smoked or barbecued meats, rye bread and certain sharp cheeses.

Reinheitsgebot: A German purity law enacted in 1516 that permits only malted barley, hops, yeast and water to be used in the brewing of beer sold in Germany. Though it has no jurisdiction outside Germany, many North American brewers follow it, and some use the fact that they meet its guidelines as part of their advertising. Since Germany's admission to the European Community, the Reinheitsgebot has not been legally binding since 1987, but German brewers still proudly follow it.

Sake: A fermented beverage that is a cousin to the family of fermented beverages we call beer. Sake originated in Japan where it is an important national drink. Several sake breweries have existed in both California and Hawaii over the years, but the only remaining American commercial sake brewery is in Hawaii. Sake is brewed from unmalted rice and is not hopped. The resulting substance is clear and has a 14 to 16 percent alcohol content. In contrast to beer, which is drunk either chilled or at room temperature, sake is warmed before drinking.

Steam Beer: A term that originated in San Francisco during the gold rush era to refer to beer that was produced with bottom-fermenting yeast but fermented at 60 degrees F to 70 degrees F (15 degrees C to 21 degrees C) rather than the temperatures required for true lager fermentation. Fermentation was allowed to continue in the kegs and the escaping carbon dioxide that resulted from the tapping of the kegs is the possible source of the term 'steam' beer. In any event, the term steam beer is now a registered trademark of The Anchor Brewing Company of San Francisco.

Stout: A dark, heavy, top-fermented beer popular in the British Isles, especially Ireland (where Guinness Stout is more popular than Budweiser lager is in the United States). It is similar to porter, though less sweet. Its alcohol content ranges from four to seven percent.

Stout is a dark, creamy beer produced with top-fermenting (ale type) yeast. Stout is the prominent beer type in Ireland and is widely available in England. Also brewed occasionally by microbreweries in the United States, it is not nearly so popular in continental Europe. Guinness, brewed in Dublin and London, is the definitive stout of the Irish type. It is also brewed under license in many places throughout the world.

English brewers, such as Samuel Smith in Tadcaster, also produce oatmeal stout in which oats are used along with barley malt.

Tesguino: A type of corn beer produced by the Indians of Mexico and the American Southwest prior to their contact with Europeans.

Wheat Beer: Beer, by definition, is a beverage derived from malted barley. Other grains, such as rice and cornmeal, are often used in less expensive, mass market brands as a cheaper source of starch, but this practice is frowned upon by discriminating brewers and consumers. Exceptions are made in the case of oats in English oatmeal stout and with wheat in American wheat beer, German **weissbier** and Flemish **witbier**. Both the German and Flemish terms are literally translated as meaning 'white' beer. This is a reference to the light color of the beer and the fact that it usually has yeast particles in suspension and hence it is cloudy, transluscent and lighter in appearance than if it were transparent. In Germany, weissbiers that are cloudy are identified with the prefix *hefe* (yeast) as hefeweissbier, or simply hefeweiss.

Weissbier: A German word literally meaning beer that is white (weiss), but actually implying a style of pale-colored, top-fermented beer made with about half wheat malt. It is typical of Berlin and northern Europe. A **hefeweissbier** is a weissbier in which yeast sediment remains in suspension in the beer. Weissbier is also known as **weizenbier**, but should not be confused with **wiesenbier**, which is a festival beer that may or may not contain wheat malt.

Witbier/Bière Blanche: Flemish/French literally meaning white (wit/blanche) beer. It is brewed using over half wheat malt. A cousin to German weissbier, witbier is indigenous to the northern, Flemish-speaking areas of Belgium.

Wort: An oatmeal-like substance consisting of water and mashed barley in which soluble starch has been turned into fermentable sugar during the mashing process. The wort is cooked, or brewed, in the brew kettle for more than an hour and for as much as a day, during which time hops are added to season the wort. After brewing, the hopped wort is filtered and fermented to produce beer.

Yeast: The enzyme-producing one-celled fungi of the genus *Saccharomyces* that is added to wort before the fermentation process for the purpose of turning fermentable sugar into alcohol and carbon dioxide.

BELOW: Peroni's high-speed bottling line in Rome.

INDEX

Note: Please refer to the relevant maps within each chapter to locate the major breweries, and refer to the Glossary for items not mentioned in the Index.

Picture Credits